THE BEDFORD SERIES IN HISTORY AND CULTURE

Christopher Columbus and the Enterprise of the Indies

A Brief History with Documents

Geoffrey Symcox

University of California, Los Angeles

and

Blair Sullivan

University of California, Los Angeles

D0140935

BEDFORD/ST. MARTIN'S   Boston ◆ New York

For Bedford/St. Martin's

Executive Editor for History: Mary V. Dougherty
Director of Development for History: Jane Knetzger
Developmental Editor: Carina Schoenberger
Production Supervisor: Jennifer Wetzel
Senior Marketing Manager: Jenna Bookin Barry
Project Management: Books By Design, Inc.
Text Design: Claire Seng-Niemoeller
Indexer: John R. Jenson
Cover Design: Billy Boardman
Cover Art: King Fernando Surveys the Indies. From *The History of the Discovery of the New Indian Islands of the Canaries: A Selection from the Repertorium Columbianum,* copyright © 1989 by the Regents of the University of California.
Composition: Stratford Publishing Services, Inc.
Printing and Binding: Haddon Craftsmen, an RR Donnelley & Sons Company

President: Joan E. Feinberg
Editorial Director: Denise B. Wydra
Director of Marketing: Karen Melton Soeltz
Director of Editing, Design, and Production: Marcia Cohen
Manager, Publishing Services: Emily Berleth

Library of Congress Control Number: 2004107918

Manufactured in the United States of America.

0   9   8   7   6   5
f   e   d   c   b   a

For information, write: Bedford/St. Martin's, 75 Arlington Street, Boston, MA 02116 (617-399-4000)

ISBN: 0-312-41021-2 (paperback)
        1-4039-6807-1 (hardcover)
EAN: 978-0-312-41021-6

Acknowledgments

   Excerpts from volume 2 of the *Repertorium Columbianum,* courtesy of Professor Helen Nader, University of Arizona.
   Excerpts from volume 3 of the *Repertorium Columbianum,* courtesy of the UCLA Center for Medieval and Renaissance Studies.
   Excerpts from volumes 4 through 12 of the *Repertorium Columbianum,* courtesy of Brepols Publishers, Turnhout, Belgium.
   Excerpts from *Diego Alvarez Chanca, Medico di Cristoforo Colombo,* courtesy of the Consiglio Nazionale delle Ricerche, Cagliari, Italy.

Foreword

The Bedford Series in History and Culture is designed so that readers can study the past as historians do.

The historian's first task is finding the evidence. Documents, letters, memoirs, interviews, pictures, movies, novels, or poems can provide facts and clues. Then the historian questions and compares the sources. There is more to do than in a courtroom, for hearsay evidence is welcome, and the historian is usually looking for answers beyond act and motive. Different views of an event may be as important as a single verdict. How a story is told may yield as much information as what it says.

Along the way the historian seeks help from other historians and perhaps from specialists in other disciplines. Finally, it is time to write, to decide on an interpretation and how to arrange the evidence for readers.

Each book in this series contains an important historical document or group of documents, each document a witness from the past and open to interpretation in different ways. The documents are combined with some element of historical narrative—an introduction or a biographical essay, for example—that provides students with an analysis of the primary source material and important background information about the world in which it was produced.

Each book in the series focuses on a specific topic within a specific historical period. Each provides a basis for lively thought and discussion about several aspects of the topic and the historian's role. Each is short enough (and inexpensive enough) to be a reasonable one-week assignment in a college course. Whether as classroom or personal reading, each book in the series provides firsthand experience of the challenge—and fun—of discovering, recreating, and interpreting the past.

Natalie Zemon Davis
Ernest R. May
Lynn Hunt
David W. Blight

Preface

Columbus is a historical figure of incontrovertible importance. He was long hailed as the "discoverer" who brought Christianity and European civilization to the American continent. But political and cultural developments, particularly the breakup of European colonial empires after World War II, led scholars to raise serious questions about Columbus's motives and methods, and about the impact of Spanish colonization on the indigenous peoples of the Americas. Although they still recognize the unparalleled historical significance of his voyages, and pay tribute to the courage and technical skill that made them possible, most scholars today have adopted a more critical stance toward Columbus and what he did. As editors of the *Repertorium Columbianum,* a multivolume collection of contemporary sources bearing on Columbus's voyages, we have set out to convey to a nonspecialist audience some of the results of the current scholarly debates and recent research on Columbus and his voyages.

The introduction to this volume provides a narrative of Columbus's extraordinary career. Born to a humble family in the great mercantile city of Genoa, Columbus went to sea at an early age. A decade of residence in Portugal perfected his seafaring skills and planted the seed of his plan to sail west in search of a shortcut to the fabled wealth of Asia. In 1492, as every schoolchild knows, he secured support from the Spanish monarchs for his venture, sailed across the Atlantic, and reached a group of islands, which he claimed for the Spanish crown. Believing he had reached the eastern coast of Asia, he mistakenly named them the "Indies," and their inhabitants "Indians."

Columbus's voyage marked the beginning of what would come to be called Spain's "Enterprise of the Indies"—the colonization and evangelization of the new lands. In 1493 the Spanish crown sent Columbus on a second voyage to establish a permanent settlement in the Indies. But the new colony was soon beset by dire problems: disease, famine,

strife among the settlers, and warfare against the indigenous population. For the inhabitants of the Indies, the arrival of the Europeans
was catastrophic. It disrupted their traditional way of life and con-
demned them to extinction within a few decades. Columbus did nothing to prevent the colonists' brutal exploitation of the indigenous
population; in fact, he actively participated in it. Meanwhile he embarked on another voyage of exploration in 1498 and became the first
European to reach the South American continent, giving further proof
of his brilliance as a navigator. But as a colonial governor he proved a
failure, and the Spanish monarchs recalled him in disgrace in 1500.
They still prized his nautical skills, however, and sent him on another
voyage of exploration in 1502–4, in the course of which he reached
the coast of Central America. Columbus died in 1506, bequeathing to
his sons the titles and the wealth he had accumulated as the reward
for his exploits.

The introduction concludes by examining the controversies that
have grown up around Columbus and the impact of his voyages, trac-
ing how his reputation has waxed and waned, especially in the United
States. The introduction also includes a table listing the main crops,
animals, and diseases that were exchanged among Eurasia, Africa,
and the Americas after 1492 in the so-called Columbian Exchange.
This was perhaps the most important—although unintended—consequence of the contact that Columbus initiated between what Europeans soon came to call the "Old World" and the "New." In addition,
the introduction includes a genealogical table of the Columbus family
and several maps depicting the voyages Columbus undertook.[1]

Following the introduction is a series of contemporary documents
that describe Columbus and his four voyages. These documents in-
clude excerpts from the log of his first voyage and a wide variety of
other materials: official documents like legal records relating to his
family's activity in Genoa, his agreements with the Spanish crown, and
papal bulls demarcating the nascent colonial empires of Spain and Portugal; accounts of Columbus's three later voyages, some by eyewit-
nesses; the first European descriptions of the Indies, of their flora and
fauna, of their inhabitants and their culture; and judgments by contemporaries on Columbus and his achievements.

A vast range of materials has been unearthed and analyzed since
serious scholarly research on Columbus and his voyages began two

---

[1]Place names appear in Spanish where applicable, for consistency with the names
used in the documents.

centuries ago. We have selected the sources included here to give an idea of the wealth of documentation that exists for studying the man and his career. To make the documents easily intelligible, we provide short commentaries that situate them in their context and gloss notes that explain any obscure terms they may contain. Our aim is to present a balanced view of Columbus and his achievements. We hope our readers will evaluate these documents for themselves and come to their own conclusions about the nature, purpose, and impact of Columbus's voyages, always remembering that research continues, that interpretations constantly change, and that there are no final, definitive answers to the questions the documents raise. Concluding this volume are a chronology to help readers follow Columbus's life and his four voyages, a glossary of terms, a list of questions for further consideration, and a selected bibliography of primary and secondary sources related to Columbus.

ACKNOWLEDGMENTS

We must record several debts of gratitude to those who have helped us in writing this book. First, to the press for their careful editorial work on the manuscript, and especially to Carina Schoenberger, developmental editor, and Emily Berleth, production manager. Second, to the eight outside reviewers who offered many helpful criticisms and suggestions for improving it: James Axtell, College of William and Mary; Paul Cullity, Keene State College; Paul W. Mapp, College of William and Mary; Helen Nader, University of Arizona; Anthony Pagden, University of California, Los Angeles; William D. Phillips Jr., University of Minnesota; Jim Ross-Nazzal, Montgomery College; and Roger Schlesinger, Washington State University. Finally, to the members of Geoffrey Symcox's undergraduate seminar on Columbus in Winter Term 2004 at UCLA, who read the manuscript and offered many useful criticisms of it from the viewpoint of the student audience for whom it is intended. To all of them, our sincere thanks.

Geoffrey Symcox
Blair Sullivan

Contents

Maps and Illustrations

PART ONE

Introduction: Columbus — The Man, the Voyages, the Legacy

We have all heard of Christopher Columbus. Everyone knows that he led three small Spanish ships across the Atlantic in 1492 and reached the West Indies. October 12, the date of his landing there, is celebrated as a holiday in the United States, where he ranks as a national hero on a par with the most revered presidents and civic leaders. Although he is famous throughout Europe and Latin America, only in the United States is he accorded special honor as one of the nation's founders: Every schoolchild there is taught the date of his voyage and the names of his ships. But the significance of his voyage resonates far beyond the United States: It was a decisive turning point in the history of the entire world. It represented the real start of European colonization in the Americas; the earlier Viking settlements in North America had quickly withered away. The voyage completely changed European notions of geography and confronted Europeans with a host of alien peoples and cultures, forcing them to reappraise their notions of what constituted a civilized society. It marked the most critical moment in European overseas expansion, for it united Eurasia, Africa, and the Americas in a single world system for the first time, inaugurating the global era in which we live today. Columbus's intrepid voyage across uncharted seas, and the momentous consequences that flowed from it, have made him a historic figure of mythic proportions.

Yet, a closer look soon reveals that Columbus is a far more complex, ambiguous, and controversial figure than the heroic icon made familiar in the United States by school textbooks, films, national holidays, and popular song. It is important to remember that perceptions of him have shifted over time, and that they continue to change. Scholarly investigation into Columbus's life and explorations, based on archival documents, began with the researches of the Spanish historian Martín Fernández de Navarrete (1765–1844) in the early nineteenth century. Since that time historians have discovered many new documents that have added to our knowledge of the explorer's career and altered our conception of it. This conception has also changed because of shifts in our political and moral horizons, especially as decolonization gathered momentum after World War II and peoples in the non-European world regained their independence and cultural identities. Today we no longer regard Columbus in the way people did a century ago, as the inspired hero who brought civilization and Christianity to the New World. Although this view persists to some extent, historical assessments of him have become more critical. Along with his undoubted achievements as a pioneering explorer and navigator we must now consider the negative—or even catastrophic—impact of his voyages on the indigenous peoples of the Americas. This shift in perceptions can be illustrated by comparing the celebrations that honored Columbus in Europe and the Americas in 1892 with the more muted commemorations—*celebrations* is perhaps too strong a word—staged for the quincentenary of his voyage in 1992. The earlier festivities, notably the Columbian Exposition at Chicago, came at the high point of European (and United States) colonial domination, and expressed optimism and confidence in manifest destiny and the white man's mission to civilize the globe. But by 1992 this self-confident tone had largely vanished. Columbus, the hero of 1892, was now seen by many as a villain. He was still praised for his skill as a master mariner and explorer, but he was no longer hailed as the bearer of civilization and Christianity to a benighted continent; instead he was denounced by some as the man who brought slavery, smallpox, and slaughter to the Americas. Over the past century the wheel has turned full circle, and any appraisal of Columbus—such as this one—must take this drastic reevaluation into account.

Any historical assessment of Columbus must also seek to present the man and his achievement in their full complexity as revealed by almost two centuries of scholarly research, whose fruits rarely find their way into the textbooks. The traditional picture is oversimplified and incomplete: It omits the long apprenticeship that enabled Columbus to acquire the geographical knowledge and seamanship without which he could not have undertaken his voyage; it focuses on his first voyage and glosses over his three subsequent voyages to the Americas in 1493, 1498, and 1502, each with a different purpose and each of great significance in its own right; it pays far too little attention to his actions as governor of the colony he established in 1493 on the island of Hispaniola (today Haiti and the Dominican Republic), which laid the foundations of the Spanish imperial system in the New World and set the pattern for the colonists' relations with the indigenous peoples; it has nothing to say about the reaction of those peoples to Columbus and the Spanish colonists or about the disasters unleashed by European settlement among them; it oversimplifies and distorts Columbus's relationship to the Spanish crown; it says little or nothing about the webs of political patronage and private financial support that helped make his enterprise possible. In some ways it is actively misleading, for it contains elements of legend or even outright fabrications calculated to enhance the glory of Columbus as navigator and leader of men but unsupported by historical evidence of any kind. Scholars continue to argue over the basic facts of his life, over the motives behind his voyages, and over their world-shattering consequences, but little of this debate finds its way into the popular record. School textbooks continue to repeat hoary legends about Columbus that research has long discredited. The purpose of this book is to bring some of the sources of this scholarly research and debate to the attention of a wider audience in order to add depth and complexity to the shallow, one-dimensional, partly fictional image of Columbus that is still current.

COLUMBUS'S GENOESE ORIGINS AND EARLY LIFE

Documents in the archives of the city of Genoa show that Christopher Columbus—or Cristoforo Colombo—was born there in 1451 (Documents 1 and 2; see Figure 1). He was the eldest of at least five children; two of his brothers, Bartolomeo and Giacomo (or Bartolomé and Diego Colón as they came to be known in Spain), would later play key roles in his explorations and colonial enterprises. Family solidarity was an important factor in Columbus's career: Two cousins, Giovanni and Andrea, also served him on his later expeditions to the Indies. His family was of humble origin and had only recently immigrated to

Figure 1. *Columbus's Family Tree.*
Columbus was born as Cristoforo Colombo in the city of Genoa.

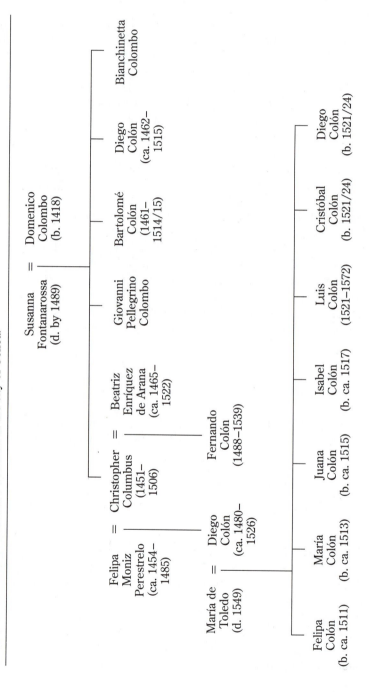

Genoa from the countryside via the nearby port of Savona. His father, Domenico, a weaver by trade, also kept a tavern and owned some parcels of farmland outside the city; at the time of Columbus's birth he held a minor post as the keeper of one of Genoa's city gates, thanks to the patronage of the powerful noble clan of the Fregoso, then dominant in Genoese city politics. The support of influential Genoese families like them was of great value to Columbus throughout his career, as we shall see.

Columbus never forgot his Genoese origins. Although he spent his later life in Spain, he never adopted Castilian citizenship, despite the advantages it would have brought. In a letter he wrote in 1502 from Spain to the directors of Genoa's state bank, the Banco di San Giorgio, he asserted his continuing loyalty to his native city: "Though my body is here, my heart is always with you." His fellow citizens reciprocated these feelings; contemporary Genoese chroniclers took pride in recording his achievements, which they believed conferred glory on their city (Document 9). Columbus's youth was spent in this bustling mercantile city-state, and these formative years were decisive. He was educated in a grammar school run by his father's guild, where he learned reading and writing, arithmetic, and Latin. This constituted all his formal education; contrary to some accounts, he did not attend the university of Pavia in northern Italy. His schooling did not last long, for at a relatively early age he went to sea as a merchant's apprentice and then as a sailor aboard Genoese ships plying the Mediterranean. Here he began to learn the craft of seamanship that was the foundation of his later achievements.

His city of Genoa lived by trade (see Figure 2). Hemmed in by mountains, with very little agricultural land, the city was oriented toward the sea. It stood at one of the main commercial crossroads in the western Mediterranean; from its port, trade routes threaded their way inland over the mountains to northern Italy, central Europe, and France. Genoese ships sailed the length and breadth of the Mediterranean, to the north African coast, and into the Black Sea. Westward they ranged as far as Britain and the Low Countries. Since the fourteenth century Genoese merchants had been active in Spain and Portugal, establishing branches of their firms in Lisbon and Seville, where their wide-ranging connections and advanced business skills gave them a central role in local commerce. They were closely linked to the Portuguese and Spanish crowns, loaning them money and acting as their financial agents. This well-connected network of Genoese merchants in the Iberian states was of critical importance to Columbus: He worked as an agent

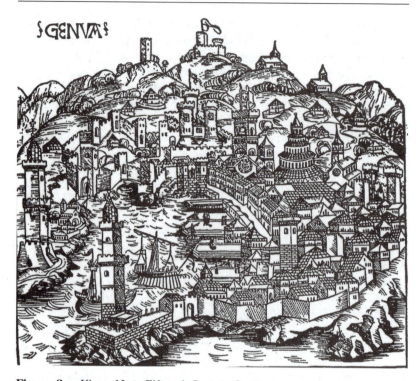

Figure 2. *View of Late Fifteenth-Century Genoa.*
Source: From Hartmann Schedel, *Liber Chronicarum,* Nuremberg, 1493.

for Genoese merchants in Lisbon in the 1470s (Document 2); a wealthy Genoese merchant at Seville, Francesco Pinelli, was one of the financial backers of his voyage in 1492; and further capital was invested by other Genoese (and also Florentine) merchants residing there.

Columbus's early years in Genoa also instilled in him the mercantile attitudes that guided him throughout his career. *Januensis ergo mercator* ("Genoese, and therefore a merchant") said the old proverb, and Columbus proved true to his commercial heritage. From the documents in the Genoese archives we know that as a young man he engaged in small-scale commercial ventures, either for his father or on his own account. Throughout his life his outlook was that of a businessman, alert to any opportunity for profit. The Log of his first voyage (Document 12) notes not only the gold he found but also the different plants he identified, which he thought might be of commercial value—mastic, used in the textile industry; aloes, for medicinal purposes; various kinds of spices; cotton; and so on. (Most of his identifications proved wrong, however.) The settlements he established at La Navidad in 1492, or at Isabela a year later, or which he tried to found on the coast of Veragua in 1503, were conceived very much like typical Genoese trading posts, perched on the periphery of their host communities, living solely by commerce with them. And after the settlement at Isabela began to languish and the meager deposits of gold on the island of Hispaniola began to run out, Columbus turned to an alternative source of profit: Indian slaves. He shipped his first consignments to Spain in 1494 (Document 14). That Columbus would have inaugurated the American Indian slave trade is in no way surprising, for he was simply continuing a common practice in the Mediterranean world: A slave trade had existed there for centuries, and Genoese merchants were leaders in it, shipping captives from the Black Sea to sell in Italy and the Muslim countries.

COLUMBUS IN PORTUGAL, 1476–1485

Columbus's Mediterranean apprenticeship, nautical and commercial, ended in August 1476, when the Genoese ship on which he was serving was wrecked on the coast of Portugal. He spent the next decade or so of his life in Portugal, and this phase of his experience was as crucial for his later career as his formative years in Genoa were. Despite its small size and meager population, under the leadership of the royal family and the merchant communities in its port cities, Portugal had become the pioneer among the European states in Atlantic exploration. Portuguese fishermen sailed far into the Atlantic and Portuguese merchants had long frequented the ports of northern Europe and the Mediterranean: Now they were venturing westward to the Atlantic islands and south along the coast of Africa in search of gold, ivory, pepper, and slaves. Profiting from this experience, Portuguese mariners and navigational experts were steadily improving the technology of oceanic sailing. By the time Columbus arrived in Portugal, local shipwrights had developed two types of sailing ship, the caravel and the nao, capable of long-distance oceanic voyages. They were equipped with a combination of square and lateen (or triangular) sails that allowed them to tack and maneuver even in unfavorable winds. In 1492 Columbus used these two types of ship: The diminutive *Pinta* and *Niña* were caravels, the larger *Santa Maria* a nao. The mariner's compass was in general use, and Portuguese navigators were working out a method for calculating latitude by using an astrolabe or cross-staff to measure the angle of the sun above the horizon at midday. In 1484 King João II of Portugal assembled a group of mathematicians, led by the Jewish scholar José Vizinho, that produced a manual of tables correlating the angle of the sun with the degree of latitude, which allowed a mariner to sight the sun and then read his position with far greater accuracy than ever before.

These technological advances were part of a program of oceanic exploration that had started in the early fifteenth century with territorial conquests in Morocco and tentative voyages south along the African coast and westward to the islands of Madeira and the Azores. As new information came in, Portuguese cartographers, often sponsored by the crown, drafted maps of the coastline, islands, and oceanic space of the Atlantic. By mid-century Portuguese settlers were colonizing Madeira and the Azores, where they established farms and sugar plantations, anticipating the colonization Columbus would initiate in the Caribbean after 1493. By then Portuguese traders were bringing cargos of gold, ivory, and slaves from West Africa to Lisbon, and in 1471 the crown set up a permanent trading post at São Jorge da Mina (or Mina, "gold mine") on the coast of what is today Ghana. Meanwhile a series of Portuguese expeditions was pushing south along the African coast, until in 1487–1488 the one led by Bartolomeu Dias rounded the Cape of Good Hope, sailed into the Indian Ocean, and returned safely to Portugal, thus opening the sea route from Europe to India.

Once settled in Portugal, Columbus perfected his skills as a mariner, drawing full benefit from the knowledge that Portuguese sailors and colonists were accumulating of the Atlantic, its wind systems, currents, and islands. We know that he made at least one voyage to Madeira (Document 2), and that he resided there for a time; he claimed to have sailed to England, Ireland, and even as far north as Iceland, and to have visited Mina, perhaps in 1482. But more important, in about 1479 he married Felipa Moniz Perestrelo, the daughter of the ex-governor of Porto Santo, one of the islands in the archipelago of Madeira. She bore him a son, Diego, but died within a few years, probably by 1485. Felipa came from a noble family whose connections had helped her father secure his Atlantic governorship. How a woman of this elevated social class came to marry a commoner like Columbus remains a mystery, but the marriage placed him at the center of the expanding enterprise of Portuguese Atlantic trade and colonization. Information from the Perestrelo family and his voyages to Madeira and the other Atlantic islands would have opened his eyes to the possibility that yet other islands might exist further to the west. Contemporary maps, drawn according to the geographical scheme of Ptolemy of Alexandria (2nd c. CE), showed no landmass between the west coast of Europe and the east coast of China (see Figure 3). The Americas did not appear on these maps, which showed no continent blocking the way from Spain to Cathay, but merely a scattering of islands, with Cipangu (Japan) closest to China. Columbus's speculations were probably fed by the tales of sailors who had ventured beyond the Azores and claimed to have seen signs of land to the west. Such stories may be at the root of the legend of the "unknown pilot" who was supposedly blown by a storm to the far shores of the Atlantic and returned, dying, to recount what he had seen to Columbus (Document 4).

Not all of Columbus's time in Portugal was spent in Atlantic voyages, however. He also resided in Lisbon, apparently making his living as a dealer in books and maps, along with his brother Bartolomé, a skilled geographer and mapmaker, who joined him there at some point. In Lisbon, the nerve center of Atlantic exploration, Columbus had the opportunity to study the most up-to-date maps and to read widely in the cosmographical and geographical literature, from classical authors like Ptolemy to near-contemporaries like Pierre d'Ailly (1350–1420), which was becoming available through the new medium of print. This reading fed his speculations about lands to the west and led him to formulate the beginnings of a theory that China could be reached by sailing westward across the island-studded ocean that separated it from Europe. By recalculating Ptolemy's estimate of the Earth's circumference, Columbus came to believe that such a voyage would not be impossibly long: He assumed (with undue optimism) that the Earth was no more than 18,000 miles in circumference (the correct figure is 24,830 miles), thus radically shrinking the distance between the two continents. His ideas were also decisively influenced by his reading of Marco Polo's (1254?–1324) account of China — or Cathay, as it was known — and its riches. (He seems to have been unaware that it was two centuries out of date: The empire of the Grand Khan whom Marco Polo served had disappeared long ago. For Columbus, Marco Polo's account still held good.) The commercial wealth and urban splendors of China, as described by Marco Polo, became a magnet that drew Columbus westward on what he assumed would be a relatively short voyage from the western extremity of the European

landmass to the eastern extremity of China. We know that this plan had taken shape by the early 1480s, because Columbus proposed it then to King João II of Portugal (r. 1481–1495), seeking his support for a westerly voyage to China. The king rejected his proposal, partly it seems because Columbus was demanding too great a share of the potential profits.

COLUMBUS IN SPAIN, 1485–1492

Columbus left Portugal late in 1485 and moved to Spain with his young son Diego. The Spanish kingdoms had long been the political and commercial rivals of Portugal, but for much of the fifteenth century they had been largely paralyzed by internal conflict, while Portugal had benefited from relative internal unity. The marriage of Fernando of Aragón and Isabel of Castile in 1469 had united the two principal Spanish kingdoms into a single monarchy, which initiated a slow process of recovery. The Catholic monarchs (as they were known) put an end to rebellion and civil war and built up the institutional structure of their state. They installed royal officials in the towns, tightened up the enforcement of public order, improved the collection of taxes, and increased the army. They also sought to increase the cultural and religious unity of their kingdoms by an attack on the minority populations of Jews and Muslims, continuing the medieval Spanish crusading tradition, the Reconquista. In 1478 they established the Inquisition to police and punish Jewish converts to Christianity who reverted to their former religion, and in 1482 they began the conquest of Granada, the last Muslim kingdom in the Iberian peninsula. The colonization of the Americas can be seen both as an extension of the Reconquista and as part of the imperial state building initiated by the dynastic union of the two crowns. Fourteen ninety-two, the year of Columbus's momentous first voyage, was also a decisive moment in the religious unification of the Spanish kingdom: Granada fell in January, closing the last chapter of the Reconquista, and on March 31 the

Figure 3. *Ptolemaic Map of the World.*
The west coast of Europe and the east coast of China stand at opposite ends of a single vast Eurasian continent. The twelve cherubs' heads indicate the principal winds and the points of the compass.
Source: From Ptolemy, *Geography,* Ulm, 1482. Reproduced by permission of the Huntington Library, San Marino, California.

Catholic monarchs decreed that their Jewish subjects must convert to Christianity or depart into exile.

Columbus arrived in Spain as this political consolidation was under way. He settled initially at the port of Cádiz while he continued his search for a financial backer of his plan for a westerly voyage to China: He was always a tireless self-promoter. In 1487, with the aid of the leading feudal lord in the area, the duke of Medinaceli, he went to the court of Fernando and Isabel seeking support for his scheme. They refused: They were deeply involved in the war to conquer Granada. But they employed Columbus as their agent in various negotiations (whose nature is not always clear), and he seems to have made a living too by trading in war booty and Muslim prisoners. While he was with the court at Córdoba he met a young woman, Beatriz de Arana, who became his mistress and bore him a son, Fernando, in the summer of 1488. He and Beatriz never married, perhaps because she came from a lower class; her family were artisans, and Columbus was now aspiring to move up the social scale, leaving his own artisan origins behind him. She outlived him by many years. Fernando accompanied Columbus on his last voyage and later became the historian of the Columbus family and the guardian of its papers and traditions until his death in 1539.

Meanwhile Columbus was extending his search for support beyond Spain. His brother Bartolomé went to England, and then France, in a fruitless effort to win the backing of their respective kings for Columbus's plan, and in 1488 Columbus returned to Portugal and once again put his project to João II. Again it was rejected. In historical hindsight this looks like a fatally missed opportunity for the Portuguese crown, but the king had good reason not to accept Columbus's project. His panel of experts cast grave doubts on the assumptions behind it, noting that Columbus had underestimated the distance to China. And then in December 1488 Bartolomeu Dias returned from his voyage around the Cape of Good Hope. Certain now that they had found the sea route to India and the east, João II and his advisers had no further interest in what probably seemed to them a hare-brained and risky plan.

The fall of Granada in January 1492 gave Columbus the opportunity for which he had waited and planned so long. Through the intercession of the influential community of Franciscan friars at the monastery of La Rábida, near the port of Palos, up the coast from Cádiz, he obtained an audience with Fernando and Isabel at their camp of Santa Fe near Granada. Now that Granada had fallen they could turn their attention to other projects, and although their maritime advisers expressed doubts about Columbus's plan, on April 17, 1492, they agreed to underwrite the voyage; a second agreement was signed on April 30 (Documents 10 and 11). The plan was very attractive to the Catholic monarchs because it offered them a chance to catch up with their maritime rival, Portugal, at minimal cost. They had already fought a successful war with Portugal for control of the Canary Islands in 1477–79, but they could not match the scope and success of Portuguese exploration in the Atlantic, and they were well aware of the implications of Dias's recent voyage around the Cape of Good Hope. Columbus offered them an alternate and (he claimed) shorter route to the riches of the east; if he succeeded, the Spanish crown would be able to tap that wealth more efficiently and surpass its Iberian rival in the race for trade and empire.

Taken together, the two agreements constituted a business arrangement between Columbus and the Spanish crown. They envisaged a voyage of exploration, a reconnaissance, in search of the fabled wealth of the Orient, its gold and spices. To this end, Columbus was to explore the "islands and mainland" that he might find in the Ocean Sea, the great body of water assumed to lie between Spain and Marco Polo's fabulous Cathay. The crown revived the title of Admiral of the Ocean Sea—a medieval Castilian office with broad but ill-defined jurisdiction over maritime affairs—and granted it to Columbus, along with the new title of Governor over the lands he might find. These titles, which were to remain hereditary in his family, conferred nobility on him and his descendants, an important reward for him personally. But the titles also made him an official representative of the Catholic monarchs, ensuring that any lands he might find would belong to the Spanish crown, not to him. The agreements granted him broad powers and were couched in very general terms because of the unpredictable nature of what he might find; these ambiguities later gave rise to decades of litigation between the Spanish crown and Columbus and his family (Document 19). The crown agreed to cover most of the cost of the voyage, but Columbus was permitted to invest up to one-eighth of the costs himself, with a corresponding share in the profits. Finally, it is important to emphasize that these agreements made no mention of any religious motivation for the voyage: Missionary activity among the heathens and war against Islam do not figure in the texts of the agreements, although these issues apparently figured in the discussions that led to their formulation (Document 3). Nor was there any mention of possible conquests of peoples and territories.

This was to be a commercial enterprise. Building an empire and spreading the Gospel would come later.

THE FIRST VOYAGE, 1492–1493

What came to be known as the "Enterprise of the Indies" now began to take shape. With the help of the crown's local officials, Columbus assembled his ships, crews, and provisions at the port of Palos through the summer of 1492. Most of the eighty-five men who made up the crews were recruited locally. The crown paid part of the cost of the voyage, although contrary to legend, the queen did not pawn her jewels to finance it. The town council of Palos provided the caravels *Niña* and *Pinta* to settle a penalty imposed on the town after some of its sailors had trespassed in Portuguese waters, which had caused a dispute with the Portuguese crown. These two vessels were captained by Martín Alonso Pinzón (d. 1493) and his brother Vicente Yáñez Pinzón (ca. 1461–ca. 1513), experienced mariners from Palos who played an important—though subsequently much-debated—part in ensuring the expedition's success. The town's contribution of ships and men offset part of the monarchs' share of the costs. The remaining costs were met by private investors. Columbus chartered the *Santa Maria* himself, with the financial assistance of some Genoese merchants and a Florentine trading at Seville, Juanoto Berardi, who seems to have acted as his partner. And as Columbus's vessels were making their preparations, other ships in the harbor were taking on large numbers of Jews who had chosen to flee the Spanish kingdoms rather than embrace Christianity, as ordered by the edict of March 31.

The three ships set sail from Palos on August 3, heading south to the Canary Islands, and on September 9 they left the Canaries on a west-southwesterly course (Map 1, page 38). From the knowledge of the Atlantic he had acquired during his years in Portugal, Columbus believed that the winds in that latitude would be favorable for sailing westward. His assumption was correct; on his three subsequent voyages he followed the same route via the Canary Islands. We can follow his day-to-day progress thanks to the log he kept (Document 12)—in Spanish, since Cristoforo Colombo had hispanicized himself as Cristóbal Colón—which was preserved in an abbreviated version by his biographer, the Dominican friar Bartolomé de Las Casas (1484–1566). On the night of October 11–12 land was sighted, just in time to head off a mutiny by the crew, fearful that they had gone too far west to make the homeward voyage safely. Columbus had brought his ships to what he assumed (wrongly, of course) was their intended destination—the eastern coast of Asia. In the morning he and some of his men set foot on the island of Guanahaní (probably Watling Island in the Bahamas), which he named San Salvador (Map 2, page 39). What ensued was one of the most decisive moments in human history: the first contact between two completely alien cultures on a collision course. But in itself the event was surprisingly prosaic. Columbus took formal possession of the island for the Spanish crown, in an act duly attested by the ship's secretary. Meanwhile some of the local Taino people came to greet him and his men. Columbus noted that they were handsome and physically similar to the Canary Islanders, but that they wore no clothes and had no iron implements—clear signs of material and cultural backwardness according to European notions of civilization. Relations were friendly; despite the lack of a common language, the indigenous people happily engaged in barter with Columbus's men. He noted that they seemed to have no conception of private property or of the value of the goods they bartered for the trinkets his men traded with them.

From Guanahaní Columbus took his ships on a wandering course through the Bahamas, constantly amazed by the beauty of the landscape. Along the way he captured local people to serve as guides and interpreters, following a method used by the Portuguese in their African explorations; most were released, but he brought a handful of these exotic beings back to Spain, along with parrots, artifacts, and gold nuggets, as evidence of the new lands. At the end of October the fleet encountered a large landmass, which Columbus believed to be the Asian mainland, but which was in fact Cuba. Here he dispatched his interpreter—a converted Jew who spoke Arabic and Chaldean, languages that would be understood at the court of the Grand Khan, with whom Columbus wanted to make contact. The man found no trace of the Khan, and instead of the rich cities Marco Polo had described, he came across a few villages of thatched huts. In some places the people wore gold ornaments, leading Columbus to assume with his habitual optimism that the land abounded in rich gold mines. Despite having only the most superficial understanding of the Taino language, he believed that the Tainos regarded him and his men as semi-divine and were eager to convert to Christianity. Significantly, he observed that they would make excellent servants and laborers.

He also convinced himself that the forests were full of valuable plants: cotton, mastic, aloes, cinnamon, spices. (His identifications were incorrect; none of these plants, except the cotton, would prove to be of commercial value.)

Such misconceptions recur constantly in the Log. Reading the narrative, one is struck by the degree to which his preconceptions colored Columbus's observation of the startlingly new flora, fauna, and peoples he encountered. This was of course inevitable: He could not instantly discard his cultural baggage, which was that of a pious, moderately well-educated, European merchant-sailor with a stubborn streak. As a pious Christian he naturally regarded the Tainos as idolaters, ripe for conversion to the superior truths of his own faith. And just as he insisted, in the face of mounting evidence to the contrary, that the lands he was exploring must be part of the Grand Khan's empire, so he tended to fit all the other new phenomena into his preexisting mental framework. To make sense of what he saw, he had to assimilate the unknown to the known, the new to the familiar. Take, for example, his sighting of three mermaids on his homeward voyage: They were probably manatees, creatures unknown to him, which he identified as best he could by reference to what he knew. The mental grid into which he slotted all these confusing new experiences was constructed from information about non-European cultures he had picked up on his earlier voyages and from his reading of travel literature by Marco Polo and classical authors like Pliny the Elder (23/24– 79 CE) and the tall tales of the apocryphal Sir John Mandeville (mid-fourteenth century). The result was periodic flights of fancy, exemplified by his belief that some of the islands were inhabited by Amazons. Mythical races of Amazons had peopled the European imagination since the classical era, as had the anthropophagi, or cannibals, of whom Columbus learned in the course of his voyage. These sensational reports were quickly picked up and transmitted across Europe (Documents 15 and 16). The Amazons remained elusive; Columbus never encountered any of them. In the case of the cannibals, however, the rumors were borne out by hard evidence.

But his misconceptions had another root, too. Driven by the need to report what he had seen in the best possible light in order to impress his backers, Columbus was all too eager to believe in the infinite potential for profit and religious conversion in the lands he was exploring. His inability to communicate with the indigenous people he encountered, save in a most elementary way, led him to interpret their utterances and gestures to suit his purposes. He inevitably fell prey to wishful thinking, self-delusion, and simple error: Like any European of his time, he lacked the mental equipment to deal with this strange, utterly foreign new world, and he had plenty of reasons—personal, political, religious, or financial—to gloss over the negative and stress the positive.

As the voyage proceeded amid lush landscapes and friendly people, the idea of founding a colony began to take shape in Columbus's mind. Soon after his first landing he had noted how easy it would be for a small number of well-armed Europeans to subdue the peaceable indigenous population. From Cuba he doubled back along the north coast of Haiti, which he named La Española (Hispaniola in English). There on December 25 the *Santa Maria* struck a reef and sank. Helped by the local villagers and their cacique (or chieftain) Guacanagarí, the crews salvaged much of the ship's cargo. Columbus then had a fort built from the ship's timbers, which he named La Navidad (Christmas) for the day of the shipwreck, which he quickly convinced himself had been a stroke of divine providence. In it he left thirty-nine men with orders to trade for gold with the local people, and then he set course for home with his remaining two ships, following a northerly route to take advantage of the prevailing winds.

On the voyage home Columbus drafted a short account of the lands he had explored (later known as the Columbus Letter, or Letter to Santángel). The Spanish monarchs had it published at once, in Castilian and then Latin, to establish their claim to the new lands. It was soon translated into other languages and printed in different versions all over Europe, and second-hand versions of the information in it circulated widely (Document 28). In the letter Columbus presented a rosy account of the islands, their beauty, their friendly people, and their abundant natural resources. He did this in part to demonstrate the value of his efforts in order to encourage the Spanish crown to finance further explorations and colonization. He claimed—and maintained for the rest of his life—that he had reached Asia. The indigenous people, whom he took to calling "Indians" in the belief that the islands they inhabited were the Indies, were docile and friendly, but with one dreadful exception: Toward the end of his voyage Columbus had encountered the fierce Caribs, who made war on their peaceful neighbors, enslaved them, and devoured them in cannibalistic feasts. In this first, well-publicized account of the Americas a dual image of the land and its peoples is already taking shape: of a sylvan paradise inhabited by noble savages, the innocent children of nature, whose bounties they were compelled to share with a race of inhuman monsters who preyed on them with bestial cruelty.

THE SECOND VOYAGE, 1493–1496: COLONIZATION

Driven off course by a storm and separated from the *Pinta,* Columbus brought the *Niña* to port at Lisbon on March 4, 1493 (the *Pinta* would make its landfall at Bayona in northern Spain). Here King João II questioned him closely about where he had been and concluded that he had sailed into waters belonging to Portugal. The king protested at this supposed violation to the Spanish monarchs; diplomatic relations grew tense through the summer of 1493, and for a time the two Iberian kingdoms were on the brink of war. In the meantime Columbus went on to Barcelona, where Fernando and Isabel were holding court, to receive a hero's welcome. They confirmed the privileges they had granted him the previous year and ordered that preparations be immediately started for another voyage, this time with the express purpose of colonization, building on the bridgehead at La Navidad (Document 13). The Enterprise of the Indies had become an imperial venture. A fleet of seventeen ships was assembled at Cádiz and loaded with weapons, provisions, tools, seeds, and farm animals. The aim was to re-create a Spanish township on the island of Hispaniola, provided with all the material necessities of European life. Columbus probably envisaged it as a trading post, while the Spanish crown probably saw it as a frontier settlement in the tradition of the Reconquista. A total of 1,200 or 1,300 colonists, all male, signed up for the voyage, attracted by the stories of easy wealth and compliant Indians set forth in the Columbus Letter. A few priests went too, the first Christian missionaries to the Americas. Among them was Father Ramón Pané, who wrote a description of the Tainos' religion—the first ethnographic account of an indigenous American people by a European (Document 31). Along with them went a force of about thirty soldiers. A little capsule of European civilization and material culture was about to be implanted in the New World.

Meanwhile Fernando and Isabel were enlisting the support of Pope Alexander VI (Rodrigo Borja, or Borgia, a Spaniard by birth) in their dispute with the Portuguese crown. At their request, on May 3 he issued a bull, "Inter Cetera I," affirming their lordship over the lands

Columbus had claimed for them and over others yet to be discovered, so long as they were not already subject to a Christian ruler. It aroused immediate protests from João II and was soon modified by a second bull with the title "Inter Cetera II," dated May 4 but actually promulgated in June (Document 23). Attempting to mediate between the two Iberian crowns, the pope in this bull established the famous line of demarcation from the north to the south pole, running one hundred leagues west of the Azores: All lands west of the line were to belong to Spain, all those east of it to Portugal. The idea was not in fact new: The treaty of Alcáçovas, which ended the war between Spain and Portugal over the Canary Islands in 1479, had established a similar line between their respective oceanic zones, endorsed by a papal bull. "Inter Cetera II" was therefore simply following this precedent. In September another bull, "Dudum Siquidem" (Document 25), confirmed and amplified the grant of lordship over the lands Columbus had claimed or might discover and claim in the future, as set out in "Inter Cetera I." In this way Fernando and Isabel secured the aid of the pope, as head of Christendom, to legitimate their claim to the lands Columbus had found. But in the eyes of many the papal grant was of dubious validity; many canon lawyers and theologians denied that the pope possessed the authority to grant dominion over distant, unknown lands, whether or not they were ruled by pagan princes.

In June 1493 Alexander VI issued another bull, "Piis Fidelium" (Document 24), destined to have a decisive impact on the emerging Enterprise of the Indies. It was addressed to Father Bernardo Buil, the leader of the clerics who were to sail with Columbus on the second voyage, authorizing them to carry out priestly functions in Hispaniola and ordering them to build churches and establish a clerical hierarchy there. These instructions were reiterated in the bull "Eximie Devotionis," issued in 1501 (Document 27). In this way the pope legitimized Fernando and Isabel's enterprise by defining it as a mission to spread the Christian faith. What had been conceived as a commercial enterprise was thus radically reconfigured: The religious impulse behind it, hitherto latent, was now brought to the fore. Spanish dominion over the Indies was to be justified by the pious work of evangelization. In a decade or so this nexus would crystallize into a formal institution, the *encomienda,* under which individual colonists were granted the right to dominate the Indians and exploit their labor, on condition that they instructed them in the Christian faith. Needless to say, this condition was not always observed. But there was another side to "Piis Fidelium" and "Eximie Devotionis." Albeit haltingly, they started to create a clerical presence in the Indies, and priests like Las Casas and Bishop Geraldini (Document 33) were the first to denounce the brutality of Spanish rule in the Indies and to press for the abolition of the *encomienda*.

The papal pronouncements legitimizing the Spanish claims to the Indies did not satisfy João II. To settle the long-running dispute between the two Iberian crowns over the Atlantic islands and sea routes, which Columbus's voyage had exacerbated, João II bypassed the papal court and opened direct negotiations with Fernando and Isabel. The outcome was the Treaty of Tordesillas in the following year (Document 26). It retained the principle of a line of demarcation but shifted it far to the west. Now it ran three hundred and seventy leagues west of the Azores, assigning a much greater zone of the Atlantic to Portugal but allowing free passage across it to Spanish ships sailing to and from the Americas. Because longitude could not be calculated with any accuracy, the exact location of this line remained uncertain. And an unintended consequence of moving it westward was that Brazil (where Portuguese sailors would land in 1500) would fall within the Portuguese empire, for when the treaty was signed no one imagined that a vast southern continent existed south of the islands Columbus had claimed for Spain; Columbus himself reached it on his third voyage in 1498.

The colonizing fleet set sail from Cádiz on September 25, 1493, and made landfall on November 3 well to the south of Hispaniola, at an island Columbus named Dominica, in the Lesser Antilles. His plan was to sail up this island chain, which he knew was inhabited by warlike Caribs, on his way to Hispaniola. The expedition soon came across some of the Carib villages, with evidence of cannibalism, and fought several skirmishes with bands of Caribs, as graphically related by Michele da Cuneo (Document 14). Sensational reports of the cannibals—and the supposed Amazons—began to filter back to Europe as the first ships returned from the expedition (Documents 15 and 16). On November 27 the expedition reached its destination, La Navidad on the island of Hispaniola, only to find the fort destroyed and the garrison dead. The causes of the disaster were never fully clarified: Columbus was told by Guacanagarí that the Spaniards had fought among themselves, but there was also much evidence that they had provoked their longsuffering Taino hosts into retaliation by their demands for gold and food and by kidnapping their women. But whatever the cause, the destruction of La Navidad and its garrison was a grim harbinger of what would soon occur on a far larger scale.

Columbus now chose a site on the north coast of Hispaniola and founded a town, which he intended to be the nucleus of the new colony. He named it Isabela in honor of the queen. The foundations were laid for a church, and the colonists built huts in which to live, but the plan for an agricultural settlement soon went badly awry. Many colonists sickened and died, for the site was unhealthy. European crops did not grow well in the tropical climate and food soon became scarce: The colonists came to depend on what they could obtain from the local population and on intermittent shipments of supplies from Spain, for transatlantic traffic was beginning as Spanish (and Italian) merchants attempted to profit from the new colony. But most of the colonists were not interested in tilling the soil, because they considered manual labor demeaning: Enticed by tales of instant wealth, they had come to the Indies to make their fortunes and live like hidalgos. Their steel weapons, armor, horses, fighting dogs, crossbows, and firearms, and the experience some of them had acquired in the Moorish wars gave them a crushing military superiority over the Tainos, who were poorly organized and armed only with bows and clubs. The Spaniards forced the Tainos to provide them with food and seized their women. Meanwhile Columbus sent armed expeditions into the interior of the island to search for gold, but the results proved disappointing. There were deposits of alluvial gold in the rivers, but the "great mine" or mother-lode from which Columbus believed they originated could not be found. He had become the victim of his earlier overoptimistic predictions. To secure a regular supply of gold, he established forts in the hinterland, whose garrisons forced the Indians to dig and pan for gold. A year later he imposed a formal system of tribute on them, demanding a quota of gold from each adult every few months. The colonists were now systematically preying on the local Taino population. Relations between them, at first amicable, rapidly deteriorated into open conflict.

Leaving the new colony under the command of his brother Diego, who had accompanied him on this voyage, Columbus set out late in April with three ships to continue the exploration of Cuba he had started on his first voyage. In an impressive feat of navigation he sailed along the island's southern coast, briefly detouring south to Jamaica. He assumed, as before, that he was exploring the coast of Asia and tried to quell growing doubts about the truth of this assumption by forcing his crews to swear that they were in Asian waters. He returned to Isabela late in September 1494 to find the colony in a state of uproar. He resumed command of the colony; his brother Diego had proved ineffectual as governor, but he fared no better himself. Columbus was a brilliant navigator, but he had no talent for politics or administration, and he could not reverse the downward spiral of events. Goaded by the colonists' exactions, the Indians were now in open revolt, and in the interior of the island fighting raged between them and Spanish war parties. At Isabela rebellion was in the air: The colonists had split into hostile factions, united only in their dislike of the Columbus brothers. In letters home to Spain they denounced them as "tyrants"; the brothers' Italian origin no doubt played its part in generating this enmity. The unrest in the colony and the barrage of criticism from the disgruntled settlers eventually undermined the favor Columbus enjoyed with the Spanish sovereigns, leading them to order an enquiry into his conduct in 1495.

But the colony's fundamental problems were too great for Columbus, or perhaps any leader with his limited means and resources, to solve. It had been founded on hopelessly unrealistic assumptions— ironically derived from Columbus's own reports. Disappointed in their expectations of instant wealth and confronted instead by famine, disease, and a hostile population, the colonists directed their resentment at one another and at their leader. Their most pressing problem, however, was food; the colony was facing a subsistence crisis. The plan to farm the land had failed, and the indigenous population could not make up for the shortage of food. The Taino were a stone-age people who lived by a mixture of farming, hunting, and fishing. Their agriculture, based on the staple crops of maize, cassava (or manioc), and sweet potatoes, could only produce a meager surplus that was insufficient to feed both them and the colonists. The result was starvation among the Taino, mass flight, and in some instances suicide to escape the colonists' demands.

To make the colony profitable, Columbus decided to exploit the only economic resource immediately available: Hispaniola's human population. Early in 1494 he had shipped twenty or so captives to Spain for sale as slaves, and later in the year he ordered a wholesale roundup to provide another shipment. Well over a thousand Indians were captured, and roughly half of them were loaded aboard ships and sent to Spain. Columbus allowed the colonists their pick of the captives who remained behind; Michele da Cuneo described the panic and terror of Taino mothers abandoning their infants in their desperation to escape. Many of the captives shipped to Spain died on the voyage; those who survived were sold to the merchants of Cádiz and Seville. Thus began the trade in American Indian slaves, which spread rapidly across the Caribbean, despite official prohibitions, for the colonists' demand for labor was insatiable. As the indigenous population of Hispaniola was wiped out by exploitation, warfare, and disease, slave-raiders extended their operations to the other islands and soon to the coast of the mainland as well.

By the middle of 1495 it was becoming clear to the Spanish crown that things were going badly wrong. The news from Hispaniola was disturbing, and the economic dividends Columbus had promised them were not forthcoming. In October a royal commission arrived to investigate, and it sent back an alarming report of mismanagement and disorder. Faced by this indictment, Columbus decided that he must return to Spain to plead his case and regain favor with his royal patrons. Leaving his brother Bartolomé, who had arrived at Isabela the previous year, to govern the colony, he sailed for Cádiz in March 1496.

THE THIRD VOYAGE, 1498–1500

After he reached Spain in June 1496 Columbus made his way to the court, accompanied by several Indians, and bearing gold and exotic presents for the king and queen. They greeted him cordially but did not give him the rapturous welcome he had received after his first voyage. The reports from Hispaniola had stimulated hostile gossip at court, where opinion was becoming increasingly critical of Columbus and his entire enterprise. Moreover, Fernando and Isabel had far more pressing concerns than the difficulties facing their small, precarious outpost across the Atlantic: They were embroiled in a war with France, fighting for control of southern Italy. In April 1497 they finally gave orders (Document 17) for another voyage to the Americas, but the preparations went ahead slowly—in contrast to the speed with which the second voyage had been organized in 1493.

The objectives of Columbus's third voyage were twofold: to carry colonists and supplies to Hispaniola, as the crown ordered, and to conduct further exploration. This latter aim seems to have been Columbus's own personal plan. About 330 colonists were recruited, some of them criminals ("with cropped ears") pardoned on condition they settle in the Indies—a sign that there was little of the spontaneous eagerness that had caused would-be colonists to flock to the expedition in 1493. Among the colonists were six women—sending them represented a major innovation in colonial policy, although the original plan had called for thirty—artisans to mine and coin the island's gold, more soldiers and priests, and a small cadre of government officials to administer the colony. Their presence showed that the crown had decided to establish tighter institutional control over the Enterprise of the Indies, whittling away Columbus's authority. The colony was no longer to be run as a virtual fief of the Columbus family, for their shortcomings were only too obvious. This assertion of authority by the crown ultimately caused a rupture with Columbus and gave rise to the litigation in which he and later his descendants sought to regain the privileges granted to him in 1492.

The expedition sailed from Sanlúcar de Barrameda, near Cádiz, on May 30, 1498, evaded a French fleet cruising off the southern Spanish coast, and reached the Canaries. It consisted of six ships in all, three of which headed straight for Hispaniola, laden with settlers, provisions, and livestock, while the other three, under Columbus's personal command, took a more southerly route to search for new lands. The Spanish monarchs were informed of recent explorations by other European powers and engaged in a race with them to find new trade routes and territories. John Cabot had sailed from England in 1497 and reached what appeared to be a great northern continent, and a Portuguese fleet under Vasco da Gama sailed for the Cape of Good Hope in July of that year: It reached India in 1498 and returned in triumph a year later. In the light of these developments Columbus's geographical conceptions were changing: He was beginning to believe either that a great continental landmass might extend to the south of the islands he had already explored, matching the landmass Cabot had found to the north, or that a sea route to China might lie somewhere to the south of them. So from the Canaries he took his three ships on a more southerly route than before, to the Cape Verde Islands, and then sailed west. On July 31 land was sighted: It was an island just off the coast of South America, which Columbus named Trinidad (Map 3, page 40).

From Trinidad the expedition sailed into a vast landlocked inlet, the Gulf of Paria. Several mighty rivers discharged into it, and the volume of fresh water flowing from them indicated that they must originate in an enormous landmass. Columbus had reached the coast of what is today Venezuela (Document 19); he and his crews were the first Europeans to sight and set foot on the South American continent. (Amerigo Vespucci [1454–1512] claimed to have explored that coast in 1497, but he falsely predated his report; in fact he reached South America a year after Columbus. Nonetheless his claim was believed at the time, and it led the German cosmographer Martin Waldseemüller to name the new continent "America" in Vespucci's honor when he published his map of the world in 1507. Despite the erroneous attribution, the name stuck.) Columbus's three ships explored the gulf and the coastline to the west, trading amicably with the Indians they met: The initial friendly encounter of 1492 repeated itself, but once again disaster followed shortly. Columbus noted that these Indians were lighter-skinned than the inhabitants of the islands and wore some clothing, suggesting to him that they were at a higher cultural level. They possessed gold ornaments and pearls, which they said they obtained along the coast to the west. To Columbus, ever optimistic, these new lands seemed rich and promising.

But they also took on a special appeal, for he now convinced himself that through divine guidance he had stumbled on the earthly paradise described in the Bible. He believed that the land and sea here sloped gradually upward to a point; the Earth, he argued, was not spherical but pear-shaped, and the tip of the pear—up which his ships were now sailing—was nothing less than the mountain of paradise described in Genesis 2:10–14. The rivers flowing into the Gulf of Paria must be the four rivers described in Genesis as flowing down from the Garden of Eden, he reasoned. These speculations are evidence that Columbus's mystical religiosity deepened in his later years. Always devoutly religious, by now he had convinced himself that his voyages were part of God's plan to spread the Gospel to the ends of the Earth, in preparation for the second coming of Christ, as foretold in the Bible. He saw himself literally as *Christo ferens,* the "Christ-bearer," a wordplay on his name that he used to sign his letters (Document 6). He urged the crown to use the wealth from the Indies to finance a crusade to recover Jerusalem from the Muslims, an idea long dear to him, as his earlier correspondence reveals. He had taken to wearing the robes of a Franciscan friar and engaging in theological disputations with monks and priests. To have found the earthly paradise seemed to him a confirmation of the divine mission on which he believed he was engaged, and he hastened to report it to Fernando and Isabel, in part perhaps too as a way of justifying his efforts and rehabilitating himself in their eyes. (We do not know how they reacted to his startling claim.) As he grew older, as his hopes dimmed and his political fortunes ebbed, it seems that he increasingly sought consolation in mystical speculation and resorted to theological and eschatological arguments to vindicate himself and his life's work.

Columbus by now had an urgent need to bolster his reputation with the crown and to refute his detractors in Spain, who were growing more numerous and more vocal as the news from Hispaniola grew worse. On August 15 he broke off his exploration of the South American coast and steered northward, in another brilliant feat of navigation through uncharted waters, to make landfall on the southern coast of Hispaniola. He arrived to find the colony's affairs in even greater turmoil than when he had left two years earlier (Document 18). His brother Bartolomé, whom he had left in charge, had lost control of the situation. One faction of colonists had rebelled against him and had established themselves in the southwest of the island under their own leaders, where they openly defied his authority. Columbus took over the governorship from Bartolomé, but he was equally unsuccessful in quelling the rebellion. He could count on the support of another faction of colonists, though their loyalty was uncertain. In an attempt to mollify the rebels, Columbus imposed a system of labor services on the caciques and their villages, requiring them to serve the colonists and provide them with food. This reduced the Indians to serfdom, anticipating the institution of the *encomienda* a few years later. Meanwhile the bitter guerrilla war continued between bands of colonists and Indians, and Columbus was powerless to stop it. In an effort to make the colony profitable, he shipped another convoy of Indian slaves to Spain, but this move produced the opposite effect from what he had intended. Queen Isabel was outraged that the Indians, who were after all her subjects, were being enslaved, and she ordered the traffic to cease. A legal loophole remained, however, which allowed the Indian slave trade to continue: It was permissible to enslave Indians defined as cannibals or captured in a war declared to be "just."

Faced with mounting anarchy and diminishing profits, Fernando and Isabel decided on a drastic step: Since Columbus had proved unable to govern the colony, he would be replaced. In the summer of 1500 a royal official, the *comendador* Francisco de Bobadilla, arrived to take command at the new capital of Hispaniola, Santo Domingo. (The capital had been moved there from the inhospitable site at Isabela a few years before, despite Columbus's objections.) Bobadilla wasted no time. He arrested Columbus and his brothers, stripped them of their authority, and dispatched them to Spain as prisoners in shackles.

THE FOURTH VOYAGE, 1502–1504, AND COLUMBUS'S LAST YEARS

Columbus was in disgrace. He had been publicly humiliated and forced to cede control of his colony to a government official. Bobadilla's takeover was an important political development: Bureaucratic government was to replace the personal rule of the Columbus family. But characteristically, Columbus made the most of his humiliation, exploiting it histrionically to recoup his lost favor. Once ashore, he refused to remove his shackles, even though permitted to do so, and wore them instead as a badge of honor. On his homeward voyage he had penned a letter of complaint and self-justification to one of his supporters at court, Juana de la Torre, the former mistress of Prince Juan's household (Document 20). In it he detailed his services to the crown, bemoaned the ingratitude and calumny he now faced, and claimed in his by-now customary mystical vein that his voyages were part of a divine plan. When Queen Isabel saw this letter, she ordered Columbus released from his fetters and summoned him to court.

Accompanied by his brothers and his two sons, Columbus presented himself before the sovereigns at Granada in December 1500. Fernando and Isabel restored his financial rights and privileges (Document 21), but understandably they did not re-appoint him governor of Hispaniola; henceforth the colony was to be run by their own bureaucrats. Slighted, Columbus initiated a campaign to regain the powers and privileges he believed were rightfully his under the various agreements he had made with the crown since 1492. His first step was to collect all these documents into a single manuscript volume, which he had copied in at least three versions; two were sent to Genoa for safe keeping (Document 6). This collection, known today as his *Book of Privileges,* furnished key evidence in the lawsuit that his son Diego filed against the crown in 1508, seeking restitution of all the powers and emoluments deriving from his titles of admiral and governor. (The crown had made these titles hereditary in the Columbus family in 1498.) This lawsuit dragged on in two major phases until 1563, finally ending in a compromise. It drew on the testimony of more than 200 witnesses, and their voluminous depositions provide a precious source for understanding the Columbian voyages (Document 19). Columbus's other strategy for rehabilitating himself employed the familiar eschatological arguments that had appeared in his writings for the past several years, but in a new form. With the help of Father Gaspar Gorricio, a Carthusian monk from Seville, he compiled a collection of texts from the Bible and medieval theologians, now known as the *Book of Prophecies,* which he addressed to Fernando and Isabel (Document 5). Using these texts, he sought to demonstrate that divine providence had directed his voyages. He had carried the Christian message to the ends of the Earth, fulfilling prophecies in the Bible and paving the way for the apocalypse and the coming of the Antichrist, which he believed were imminent.

The *Book of Prophecies* remained unfinished, however, because Columbus was soon authorized to undertake another voyage, and he abandoned the manuscript. Fernando and Isabel recognized that even though he might be a disastrously incompetent colonial administrator, he remained a brilliant navigator, and they decided to make use of his talents once again. Early in 1502 they accepted his proposal for a voyage to find a strait between the Caribbean islands and the continent of South America, which he believed would lead to the East Indies. The Spanish crown's motivation once again was its oceanic rivalry with Portugal. Vasco da Gama had returned from India in 1499 with a cargo of spices, via the long, circuitous route around the Cape of Good Hope. Columbus's plan offered the possibility of finding a shorter, more direct route to Asia—in effect like the original scheme of 1492—but modified in the light of the new geographical knowledge accumulated in the decade since his first voyage. Columbus equipped a small fleet of four ships; his principal backers were a syndicate of Genoese merchants at Seville, and one of the ships was captained by a Genoese nobleman, Bartolomeo Fieschi. On May 9, 1502, the ships set sail from Cádiz, headed south on the customary first leg of the transatlantic voyage to the Canaries, and arrived off Hispaniola on June 29. The island's new governor, Nicolás de Ovando, refused Columbus permission to land and repair his leaky ships, obliging him to ride out a hurricane in the open sea—a superb feat of seamanship (Document 22). Ovando ignored Columbus's warning of the impending storm and ordered a big convoy to sail from Santo Domingo for Spain just as the storm approached: Twenty-five vessels perished, and only three reached their destination.

From Hispaniola Columbus sailed westward to the coast of what is today Honduras. He and his crews were thus in all probability the first Europeans to explore this region of the American mainland. There they encountered Indians whose material culture seemed to them more advanced than that of the inhabitants of the West Indian islands. They wore cotton clothing and mummified their dead; they spoke of rich, thickly populated lands in the interior—the lands that Cortés conquered twenty years later—but they responded evasively to his enquiries about gold and spices. These tales rekindled Columbus's hopes that he had reached the empire of the Grand Khan. The fleet cruised southward along the coast as far as what is today Panama, bartering here and there with the local people. In January 1503 Columbus was halted by storms in the region of Veragua. He contemplated founding a trading post there, to be governed by his brother Bartolomé, who had accompanied him on the voyage, but the determined resistance of large numbers of Indian warriors soon forced him to give up the idea. By now his ships were in a very bad state, their timbers eaten away by shipworms; abandoning two ships that were no longer seaworthy, the expedition set sail for Hispaniola. But it did not reach its goal. At the end of June the two surviving ships arrived on the north coast of Jamaica, but they were too rotten to sail any further and had to be beached. Columbus and his men were marooned. They were forced to remain for a year on the island, until two of his captains, Fieschi and Diego Méndez, managed to summon help. They reached Hispaniola after an appalling voyage across the open sea in canoes paddled by Indians, many of whom died on the trip. From Hispaniola Columbus and his family members made their way home, arriving at Sanlúcar de Barrameda at the beginning of November 1504.

Columbus was now in very poor health; the privations of this last voyage had accelerated his physical decline. Knowing he would not live much longer, he made every effort to persuade the crown to restore all his privileges. His chief concern was to ensure that his son Diego would succeed to his titles and financial emoluments, according to the *mayorazgo* (or family trust, a prerogative of the nobility) the crown had permitted him to set up in 1498. He was a wealthy man, having profited from his share of the revenues from the colony of Hispaniola and his investments in numerous trading ventures to the Indies. These sources of income depended to a large degree on the maintenance of his privileges. But for several years the crown had been licensing merchants from the ports of Andalusia to trade with the Indies, undercutting what Columbus claimed were his rights to this lucrative traffic. He mobilized his friends at court to lobby on his behalf, but his political position was now less favorable: Queen Isabel, his chief supporter, had died at the end of 1504. In the early summer of 1505 he made his way with great difficulty from Seville to Segovia, where the court was then residing. Fernando received him in audience but did not grant his requests. Though now very ill, Columbus followed the king and the court to Valladolid, still hoping to secure his assent. But he hoped in vain: He died there on May 20, 1506, after dictating his last will.

Columbus did not die in poverty, as is often said; he died a rich man, and he passed his fortune on to his son Diego, who married a lady of the highest aristocratic lineage, crowning the ascent to wealth and noble rank of the weaver's son from Genoa. As Columbus had dreamed, his descendants would be titled nobles. Nor did he die scorned by an ungrateful sovereign, as is often believed. His title of admiral was not taken from him, although King Fernando would not restore him to the governorship of Hispaniola and the other "islands and mainlands" that were now falling under Spanish dominion in the Americas. Legally this was a violation of the original contract between Columbus and the crown, but in the litigation that began a few years later, the crown held firmly to its position. Fernando and his officials had no desire to allow overmighty subjects like the Columbus family to carve out power bases for themselves in the colonies. State sovereignty was threatened by the sweeping privileges originally granted to Columbus as admiral and governor, and the crown sought to annul them in order to assert its authority over its widening imperial domains. The first phase of the Enterprise of the Indies, pioneered by adventurers like Columbus, was giving way to a new phase of bureaucratic governance represented by figures such as Bobadilla and Ovando.

COLUMBUS'S LEGACY

Columbus had performed extraordinary services for the Spanish monarchs, even though these were not what he had originally planned. Paradoxically, what began as a search for a shortcut to the commercial wealth of Asia soon evolved into a headlong process of territorial conquest: What had been envisaged as a search for lucrative trading posts, on the Genoese or Portuguese model, became a continuation of the Reconquista. Nevertheless, Columbus's vision was absolutely central to the process of Spanish exploration and colonization; he gave it its initial impetus, and he played a decisive role in determining its direction. It is true that if he had not crossed the Atlantic to America, some other European navigator—Portuguese, or Basque, or Breton, or English—would have done so very soon, for by that time western Europe possessed the will, the technological means, and the financial and governmental infrastructures to undertake the voyage. Nonetheless, the fact remains that it was Columbus, and no one else, who made that fateful voyage, that his extraordinary skill as a navigator and mariner carried it to a successful conclusion, and that he undertook it with the backing of the Spanish crown, and no other. His first voyage, and the colonization that ensued, laid the foundations for a Spanish empire in the Americas. His subsequent explorations added immeasurably to the sum of geographical knowledge; his was the first expedition to reach South America and probably the first to explore the coast of Central America, always on behalf of the Spanish crown. His voyages initiated the spread of the religion, the language, and the culture of Spain to the New World, superimposing them onto the indigenous cultures and beginning the slow, complex, often painful process of ethnic and cultural symbiosis that continues today. At first the rewards of empire did not live up to Columbus's rosy predictions, but from the mid-sixteenth century the Spanish crown reaped enormous revenues from its domains in the Americas. The silver of Peru and Mexico helped make Spain the dominant military power in Europe for almost a century.

But Spanish imperial greatness was bought at an incalculable human cost. The impact of Columbus's arrival on the peoples of the Indies was catastrophic. Las Casas chronicled the atrocities and devastation inflicted by his fellow Spaniards in his *History of the Indies,* and in the chilling indictment of misrule, *A Short Account of the Destruction of the Indies,* which he presented to the Spanish emperor Charles V in 1540. Already by then the Taino population was almost extinct, wiped out by warfare, forced labor, and the alien diseases carried by the colonists. (The Caribs resisted fiercely and survived longer, but they too eventually succumbed.) The Tainos' culture perished with them: Today we know of them only through artifacts in museums and a few loan-words from their language: *canoe, hammock, hurricane, cacique, maize, tabac* (tobacco). And after Cortés landed in Mexico and Pizarro landed in Peru, the same terrible story was repeated, though with a somewhat less disastrous ending. The indigenous peoples of the mainland were more numerous, their political and social structures more advanced, so that they were better able to resist the European invasion. But on the continental mainland of America too the process of conquest and colonization set in motion by Columbus's voyages was disastrous for the indigenous peoples politically, culturally, and demographically, even if it did not result in their extermination, as it did for the Tainos.

We must consider other aspects of Columbus's legacy. Quite unwittingly, his voyages initiated a vast global exchange of plants, animals, and microbes, whose implications historians are only now beginning to grasp. Before 1492 Eurasia-Africa and the Americas constituted two separate ecosystems. Columbus's voyage began an exchange of life forms that has been partly destructive, partly productive (see Figure 4). Eurasian diseases such as smallpox and influenza, carried by sailors and colonists, decimated the Native American populations, who

Figure 4. *The Columbian Exchange.*

AMERICAS TO EURASIA AND AFRICA		EURASIA AND AFRICA TO AMERICAS	
Food Crops	*Animals*	*Food Crops*	*Animals*
Avocado	Dog (a breed of)	Apple, plum, citrus fruits, fig, peach	Cat
Beans (navy, lima, kidney, etc.)	Turkey, goose	Asian rice	Cattle, oxen
Blueberry	Guinea pig, nutria	Banana, plantain	Chicken
Cacao	Llama	Barley	Dog
Guava		Coffee	Donkey, horse
Maize (corn)	*Diseases*	Lettuce	Goat, sheep
Manioc (cassava)	Syphilis	Mango	Honeybee
Papaya		Melon, watermelon	Pig
Passion fruit		Millet	
Peanut, pecan, cashew		Oats	*Diseases*
Peppers (chile and sweet)		Okra	Bubonic plague
Pineapple		Olive	Chicken pox, smallpox
Potato and sweet potato		Onion, leek	Cholera
Quinoa		Pea, lentil, fava bean, chickpea	Diphtheria
Squashes and pumpkin		Root vegetables (carrot, beet,	Gonorrhea
Tomato		radish, turnip, etc.)	Influenza
Vanilla		Rye	Malaria
Wild rice		Sorghum	Measles
		Sugarcane	Mumps
Other Plants		Wheat	Pleurisy
Quinine		Wine grape	Scarlet fever
Sunflower		Yam	Whooping cough
Tobacco			Yellow fever
		Other Plants	
		Flax	

lacked the immunities against these diseases that many Europeans possessed. Syphilis arrived in Europe on Columbus's return in 1493, borne by his crews, and became endemic. The traffic always flowed two ways. European settlers, beginning with Columbus's colonizing voyage in 1493, brought their livestock and food plants with them. The indigenous peoples of the Americas were skilled agriculturalists, but their only domestic animals were the llama, a kind of guinea pig and a small dog for eating, and perhaps ducks and geese. The Europeans brought their complete barnyard of domesticated species to the Americas: horses, cattle, oxen, pigs, sheep, goats, chickens, dogs, and cats. The rapid proliferation of these animals in virgin lands largely devoid of predators revolutionized both the agriculture and the ecology of the Americas as native farmers adopted them for their own use, and their feral descendants spread everywhere. Europeans also brought with them their staple food crops, hitherto unknown in the Americas: wheat, barley, oats, and rye; vines and olives; apples, peaches, and other fruit trees. In 1493 Columbus also brought sugarcane, the foundation of the plantation economy that would boom in the Americas from the later sixteenth century, creating an inexhaustible demand for African slaves. In return, the colonists took American crops to Europe, and soon to Africa and Asia. Native American farmers had domesticated a rich variety of food plants, many of which provided greater nutritional value than Eurasian or African varieties. By the mid-sixteenth century maize was becoming a staple food in parts of southern Europe; by the end of the century European traders had carried maize and sweet potatoes to China and Japan, vastly increasing agricultural yields there; by then Africans were beginning to cultivate maize and manioc. Other American food crops gradually came to enrich Europe's diet: tomatoes, squashes, pineapples, chile peppers, many varieties of beans, and later, potatoes. Everywhere, the arrival of these new crops diversified agriculture, increased the food supply, and thus boosted the birthrate.

Columbus's voyage therefore had the unintended consequence of unleashing a global agricultural revolution with enormous demographic consequences. It also—again unintentionally—sparked an intellectual revolution in Europe. Scholars and theologians were forced to grapple with the unsettling questions posed by the encounter between Christian Europe and the peoples of the New World, who did not fit Europe's customary cultural taxonomies. The Indians' religion, as reported by Pané (Document 31), was puzzling, even when he sought to explain it by drawing parallels to Europe's classical myths. This was a dangerous new reality, for which Christian Europeans were not prepared. And even more unsettling, from the first they were struck by the apparently contradictory nature of America's peoples, already implicit in Columbus's first report. On the one hand, America seemed an Eden inhabited by peaceful innocents; on the other hand, a hell populated by inhuman cannibals. Both Peter Martyr and Bishop Geraldini (Documents 32 and 33) were baffled by this awful contradiction. The humanist Peter Martyr saw in Columbus's Indians the unspoiled beings of biblical or classical mythology. The virtuous old man he describes represented for him the inherent goodness of human nature, the innate sense of justice he believed was common to all humans. This virtuous savage, though ignorant of Christianity, knew instinctively that the soul was immortal. The people he ruled so benignly held their goods in common and so were not prey to the greed that afflicted civilized societies. Europe had much to learn from them. Yet close by them lived the cannibals, who represented for Peter Martyr the embodiment of bestial degradation and inhumanity. Geraldini similarly registered this conflicting image, but added a new element to it: The peaceful Indians who were his spiritual charges because he was bishop of Hispaniola had fallen victim not so much to their cannibal neighbors, but rather to the rapacious colonists—nominally Christian—who exploited and murdered them. Here Geraldini posed an issue that would perplex enlightened Europeans for centuries: Who then were the real cannibals? Who was truly civilized? Was Christianity an essential component of a civilized society? Might a society of pagans conceivably be more virtuous than a society of Christians?

COLUMBUS AFTER COLUMBUS

For his contemporaries, such as the historian and colonial administrator Fernández de Oviedo (1479–1557), Columbus was the "discoverer" of America and thus the founder of the Spanish empire. For this, Oviedo believed, he deserved unstinting praise and everlasting fame. Other Spanish writers echoed this judgment. López de Gómara went so far as to label Columbus's discovery "the greatest event since the creation of the world." In 1571 a celebratory biography of Columbus, attributed to his son Fernando, was published. It joined a swelling flood of travel narratives and collections of voyages in which the admiral's exploits figured prominently. Columbus's first voyage was coming to be defined as the pivotal moment in the unfolding epic of European overseas exploration and colonization, which was changing the course of history. Thus for Francis Bacon in the early seventeenth century the discovery of America, along with the invention of gunpowder and printing, allowed the modern world to claim it had surpassed the towering achievements of classical antiquity.

Las Casas's view of Columbus was less laudatory, but his long *History of the Indies,* written in the middle decades of the sixteenth century from personal knowledge of Columbus and his family and from long experience in the Spanish American colonies, is the most detailed account we have of Columbus's exploits. It long remained unknown, however, because it was not published until 1875. In it Las Casas presented a complex, ambivalent picture of the great navigator. He portrayed him on the one hand as the chosen instrument of God, bringing Christianity to the New World, and on the other hand as a flawed and fallible human being whose greed and selfishness had led him to enslave and kill the Indians. Columbus had brought the Gospel to America, but at the same time he had opened the way to the brutalities and excesses perpetrated by the Spanish settlers, which Las Casas spent his life documenting and denouncing.

In the late eighteenth century the figure of Columbus, venerated until then mainly in Europe, began to take on a different historical meaning in the newly independent United States, where he was co-opted metaphorically as one of the nation's founders: The Spanish explorer Cristóbal Colón began his mutation into the iconic figure of Christopher Columbus that we know today. For a time, in fact, there was a possibility that the new nation might even call itself "Columbia," but that name was eventually given only to the district that became its capital city. New towns on the frontier also chose that name, or "Columbus," as the new republic began to trace its point of origin back from 1776 to 1492. What was probably the first centennial celebration of Columbus's voyage took place in New York in 1792, with patriotic odes and speeches. A movement we might call "Columbianism" gained momentum in the United States through the nineteenth century, strengthened by the publication of Washington Irving's biography of Columbus in 1828. Irving made Columbus into a romantic hero, who forged ahead on his lonely course undeterred by ignorant naysayers and bigoted clerics. He finally achieved the triumph his genius deserved, only to die in poverty and disgrace, rejected by the ungrateful Spanish crown. Irving was not above embellishing his narrative with imaginary details to enhance his hero's determination and perspicacity; his biography seems to have originated the myth that

Columbus was the first person to realize that the world was round. (The ancient Greeks knew this, as did every educated European in Columbus's day.) Later biographers following in Irving's footsteps repeated and added to these mystifications. They felt obliged to turn their hero into an almost superhuman figure, befitting the role they were assigning to him as the first apostle of manifest destiny. Some of the legends invented by patriotic biographers in the nineteenth century still haunt school textbooks today.

Irving's biography was actually based on the scholarly research of Fernández de Navarrete, who in 1825 began publishing a series of documents on Spanish overseas exploration, in which Columbus naturally occupied a prominent place. Navarrete's research marks the real beginning of serious scholarly investigation into Columbus's career. Through the nineteenth century, research continued, and new documents were constantly brought to light. Scholars focused on Columbus as navigator and discoverer; little or nothing was said about his impact on the indigenous peoples of the Americas. In 1892, as part of the fourth Columbian centennial celebrations, the Italian government published a monumental series of volumes, the Raccolta Colombiana, which contains all the archival documents relating to his career that were known at the time. It marked a milestone in the study of Columbus. The continuing progress in archival research made it possible for historians in the United States like Justin Winsor and Henry Harrisse to take a fresh, critical look at Columbus and to begin replacing myth making with careful scholarship. Ironically, their work appeared as the triumphal mythologizing around Columbus reached its climax in the Chicago Exposition of 1893, which gathered a multitude of exhibits representing different peoples and cultures from around the world, paying homage to the spread of western civilization that he had supposedly spearheaded. At the same time, other celebratory initiatives were taking off. The Knights of Columbus, a primarily Italian-American Catholic organization founded in 1882, began pressing for October 12 to be declared a national holiday: Their efforts were crowned with success in 1938. Columbus Day is thus of relatively recent vintage. And Catholics in the United States and Europe mounted a campaign to canonize Columbus for bringing Christianity to the New World; these efforts to elevate him to sainthood, however, ultimately failed.

Such a parade of Eurocentric triumphalism is no longer possible. The quincentenary commemorations in 1992 stimulated a new wave of scholarly research and publication, notably the multivolume Nuova Raccolta Colombiana in Italy and the Repertorium Columbianum in

the United States. Their tone is very different from that of works published a century ago. Today we find it hard to think of Columbus as
the bearer of civilization and progress to an inert, barbarous continent,
or as a saintly figure motivated solely by his zeal to spread the Christian faith. Our view is different, for it is conditioned by a generation of
struggle during which the colonized peoples of the world have liber-
ated themselves from western domination. These struggles have made
us all aware of the darker side of the Columbian enterprise: the exploitation and destruction of indigenous peoples it initiated, the baleful
legacy it has bequeathed to us. Yet even so we must take care to maintain a balanced view and remember that no verdict is definitive. The
final word has not been said, and the questions will always remain
open. Writing the history of Columbus and his voyages remains a work
in progress; inevitably, the story will change with the passage of time.
The purpose of this volume is to acquaint readers with the wide variety of sources and interpretations now available for the study of the
Columbian enterprise and to encourage them to pose their own questions about the meaning of what happened when two worlds collided
in a fateful encounter on the beach at Guanahaní on October 12, 1492.

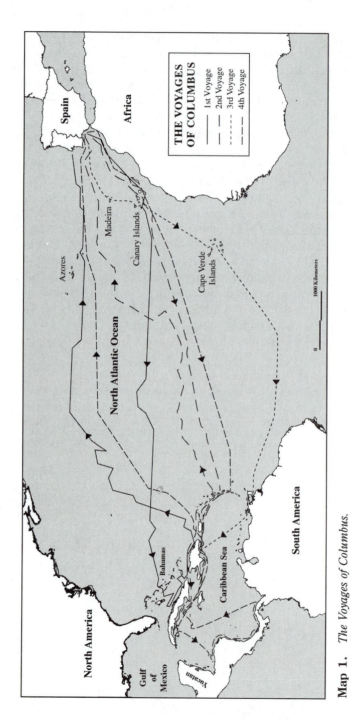

Map 1. *The Voyages of Columbus.*

This schematic overview of Christopher Columbus's four voyages to the New World illustrates the variations among his routes.

Source: Lawrence V. Mott.

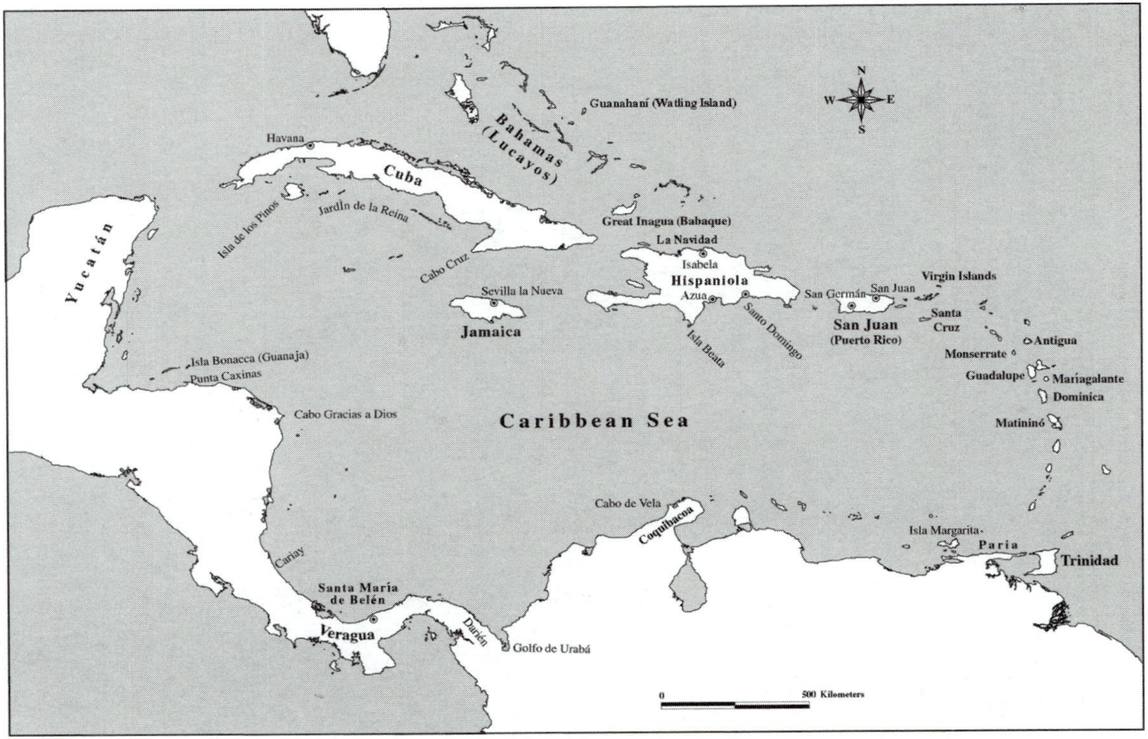

Map 2. *The Caribbean Region.*

This chart indicates principal locations mentioned in the documents pertaining to Columbus's first voyage (the Bahamas, the northern coast of Hispaniola, and the northeastern tip of Cuba), second voyage (the islands of Dominica, Mariagalante, Guadalupe, and Santa Cruz; the Virgin Islands; San Juan; Hispaniola; Jamaica; and the southern coast of Cuba), and fourth voyage (Matininó, the Caribbean coast of Central America, and Jamaica). See Map 3 for principal locations related to Columbus's third voyage.

Source: Lawrence V. Mott.

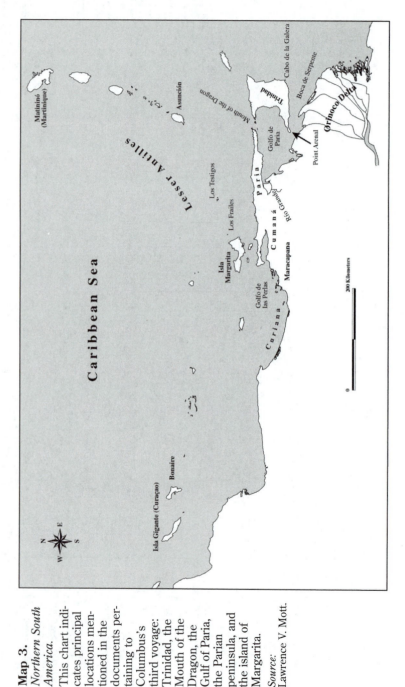

Map 3.
Northern South America.

This chart indicates principal locations mentioned in the documents pertaining to Columbus's third voyage: Trinidad, the Mouth of the Dragon, the Gulf of Paria, the Parian peninsula, and the island of Margarita.

Source:
Lawrence V. Mott.

PART TWO

The Documents

1

Christopher Columbus

1

Agreement Mentioning Domenico Colombo and His Son Christopher Columbus

Genoa, September 22, 1470

Documents 1 and 2 are notarial acts drafted in the formulaic legal terminology of the time. Although they are as dry and impersonal as legal documents of any age, they are, nonetheless, examples of the remaining documentary evidence relating to Christopher Columbus's Italian roots, the Colombo family of Liguria. In Document 1 Domenico Colombo, son of the deceased Giovanni Colombo, and his son Christopher Columbus stipulate a compromise concerning a debt in an unspecified amount contracted with Gerolamo del Porto.

In the name of the Lord, amen. Domenico Colombo, son of the deceased Giovanni, and Christopher, his son, in the presence of, and with the consent of Domenico, his father, present and consenting, as one party, and Gerolamo del Porto, son of the deceased Bartolomeo, as the other; concerning everything that one party can request and require from the other and the other from the one, up to the present day and hour, . . . they agreed and made and make a general arbitration agreement in the presence of the provident man, Lord Giovanni Agosto Goano, son of the deceased Lord Luchino, in his capacity as

John Dotson, ed. and trans., and Aldo Agosto, ed., *Christopher Columbus and His Family: The Genoese and Ligurian Documents,* Repertorium Columbianum 4 (Turnhout, Belgium: Brepols, 1998), 85–86.

arbitrator, judge, amicable compromiser, and common friend, chosen and commissioned by and between the parties and by their common agreement and will.... Which Domenico Colombo and Christopher, his son, wishing to observe in its entirety the sentence brought forth by the arbitrator and judge, promise Gerolamo, present and solemnly stipulating, to give and to pay to Gerolamo all that was decided and judged by the arbitrator and judge, terminating every objection and contradiction, and to observe exactly the sentence brought forth as above by the arbitrator and judge.

Done at Genoa, in the Serravalle Palace, namely at the bench of the Criminal Court of Genoa, in the year of the Nativity of the Lord 1470, ... Saturday, the twenty-second day of September, about the twenty-third hour.

2

Notarial Document Mentioning Christopher Columbus's Trip to Madeira to Purchase Sugar

Genoa, August 25, 1479

This important document, containing Christopher Columbus's testimony as a witness at a hearing involving the purchase of sugar on the island of Madeira, is interesting principally for Columbus's explicit declaration under oath that he is a Genoese citizen. The document also reveals that the date of his birth fell between August 26 and October 30, 1451; that he had lived in Lisbon for more than a year working for some Genoese merchants there and then returned; and that he had made a voyage to Madeira. This is Columbus's last documented stay in Genoa.

In the name of the Lord, amen. Be it known to one and all who examine the present public instrument that, appearing in the presence of me, the notary, and the witnesses inscribed below, who were especially called and invited to appear, Christopher Columbus, citizen of Genoa, was summoned here as witness and received and examined as

John Dotson, ed. and trans., and Aldo Agosto, ed., *Christopher Columbus and His Family: The Genoese and Ligurian Documents,* Repertorium Columbianum 4 (Turnhout, Belgium: Brepols, 1998), 137–40.

witness to the eternal memory of the facts at the instance and request of the noble Lodisio Centurione,[1] who wants to prove and certify the matters inscribed below.

And first he intends to prove and certify that the truth of the matter was and is that at another time in the immediately preceding year, Paolo di Negro, by commission of Lodisio himself, sent to the island of Madeira to buy a certain quantity of sugar, and Lodisio himself sent on the occasion 1,290 ducats or 1,290 *cruzados,*[2] or their value, to Paolo to buy 2,400 or more *rubbi*[3] of sugar. Christopher Columbus, by order of Paolo, was sent to the island of Madeira and there secured or bought the above-mentioned quantity of sugar, awaiting the promised money from Paolo to pay the price. But Christopher had only 103½ ducats, so that, because Paolo had not sent the required money, Christopher was not able to have the whole quantity of sugar bought and secured and was not able to load the said quantity of sugar on the ship commanded by Ferdinando Palencia, Portuguese, because of this lack of money. This was and is the truth of the matter. . . .

And this Christopher, the aforesaid witness, bodily touching the Scripture, swearing to tell and attest to the truth, said that he knows only as much as is contained in the document, namely that it was and is true that during the immediately preceding year, in the month of July, the witness himself and the said Paolo being in the locality of Lisbon, he was sent by Paolo himself to the island of Madeira to buy 2,400 *rubbi* or more of sugar; for this the witness was given by Paolo, or another for him, on the aforesaid occasion, 115,000 *reali,*[4] and then, while the witness himself was in the island of Madeira, there was sent to the witness by Paolo, or another for him, a total of 312,000 *reali,* or thereabouts, counting the 115,000 *reali.* And when the ship commanded by Ferdinando Palencia, Portuguese, landed at the island, in and on which ship he was obliged to load the quantity of sugar, he said that it was not able to be loaded, although it had been previously bought and secured by him, the witness. He could not testify in person and punctually how much of the sugar he had bought and secured since he did not have his book in which everything was distinctly

---

[1]Lodisio Centurione was a member of one of Genoa's leading mercantile families, which was active in Portugal.

[2]A *cruzado* was a Portuguese gold coin of approximately the same weight (3.5 grams) and fineness as the Venetian gold ducat, which was the international standard.

[3]A *rubbio* was a unit of dry measure (about 194.4 liters) used to weigh sugar at Madeira.

[4]The Portuguese *real* was a silver coin of about the same weight (3.5 grams) as the Venetian gold ducat.

marked and written down and to which he referred at the time of the landing of the ship; he could not himself have all the sugar bought and secured because he lacked the money that Paolo had not sent to him for payment for that sugar. . . .

Questioned concerning the source of his knowledge and in what way and how he knows the facts contained in it he answered: because the witness himself was the one against whom Ferdinando protested, and to whom he would have given his cargo if he had received the money from Paolo that was needed to pay for the quantity of sugar. . . .

Asked whether he must leave soon, he answered: yes, tomorrow morning for Lisbon.

Asked how old he is, how much he has in assets, and what side he wanted to win, he answered: that he is twenty-seven years old, or thereabouts; he has one hundred florins and more; and he wants the side which is in the right to win.

Done at Genoa, in the district of San Siro, namely in the office of the said Lodisio, in the year of the Nativity of the Lord, one thousand four hundred seventy-nine, Wednesday, twenty-fifth of August, a little past the twenty-fourth hour; in the presence of Giovanni Battista Croce, son of the deceased Gerolamo, and of Giacomo Sclavina Bernardi, citizens of Genoa, witnesses to the aforesaid, specially called and invited.

3

BARTOLOMÉ DE LAS CASAS

On Columbus's Appearance, Education, and Character

ca. 1527–1563

Bartolomé de Las Casas (1484–1576) was born into a family of merchants in Seville connected to Columbus. He arrived in Santo Domingo as a colonist in 1502; by 1510 he had become a priest and in 1511 underwent a religious conversion that led him to devote most of his long adult life to describing the atrocities that the Spanish were perpetrating

Nigel Griffin, ed. and trans., intro. Anthony Pagden, *Las Casas on Columbus: Background and the Second and Fourth Voyages,* Repertorium Columbianum 7 (Turnhout, Belgium: Brepols, 1999), 25–28.

against the indigenous inhabitants of the Americas and to fighting for their rights as free subjects of the Spanish crown. His long History of the Indies, *written between 1527 and 1563, contains the most detailed account of Columbus's life and voyages that we have, although we have very little exact information about the sources Las Casas used.*

Physically and in appearance he was tallish, above average height. His face was long and dignified, his nose aquiline, his eyes blue. His complexion was fair, ruddy in patches, and his hair and beard fair when he was young, though labor and suffering soon turned both to white. He was good-looking and lively, fair of speech and eloquent and congenial in his conversation. He was dignified and circumspect, affable with strangers, gentle and courteous with members of his own household, his mildness of manner and sensitivity to others such that those who met him quickly became fond of him. In short, his venerable appearance and noble and aristocratic bearing commanded respect; he ate and drank in moderation and was soberly dressed and shod; and when he was talking informally and was moved to laughter or to indignation, both the pleasantries and the rebukes that came to his lips were mild ones, such as "God take you!" "Does this or that not seem right to you?" or "Why did you do that and that?"

On the question of the Christian religion, there can be no doubting his Catholic faith nor that he was very devout. He was in the habit of prefacing almost everything he said or did or planned to do with the words "in the name of the Holy Trinity I shall do this" or "this will happen, or I hope that this will prove the case," and in all his letters and other writings of every sort we find him putting at the top of the page, in Latin, "Jesus and Mary guide us in the true path." I have in my possession, even as I write, quite a number of his works penned in his own hand. His favorite oath was "By St. Ferdinand!" and when he wanted to make some solemn declaration, especially when addressing a letter to the king and the queen, he would write "I hereby swear that this is the truth." He observed the fast days of the church religiously, regularly made confession and received the sacraments, kept the canonical hours as scrupulously as any priest or monk, always objected strenuously to swearing and to blasphemy, and was devoted to our Lady and to the founder of the Seraphic Order [the order of St. Francis, the "Franciscans"], St. Francis of Assisi. He was openly appreciative of the benefits the Lord bestowed upon him and it is said of him that every hour he acknowledged some fresh bounty from the Lord, much as did David in the Old Testament. When someone made him a gift of gold or of some other precious object, he would retreat into his place of prayer and, sinking to his knees, would invite all those present to join him, saying, "Let us give thanks to the Lord, who has deemed us worthy to make such great discoveries." He was everlastingly zealous of the honor of God, and imbued with a burning desire to convert these peoples that the faith of Jesus Christ should take root and multiply throughout these lands; and he was singularly moved and affected by the thought that God should have adjudged him worthy to help in some way towards the recapture of the Holy Sepulcher [the tomb of Jesus Christ in Jerusalem]. To this end, confident that God would guide him to the discovery of this promised world, he entreated her gracious majesty Queen Isabel to take a vow that all the wealth he discovered in her name would be devoted to the recapture of the Holy Land and of the holy places of Jerusalem, a vow the queen did make, as we shall recount.

He was a man of great spirit, vigor, and resolve, high minded and—to judge from what we know of his life, his deeds, and his writings—naturally inclined to lofty enterprises and to the achievement of great goals; he was patient and could endure great hardship (as will become clear in the course of our history); he forgave those who did wrong against him, asking only, it is said, that those who had wronged him recognize the error of their ways and thus might be taken back into the fold; and he was steadfast and endowed with resolution in the face of the barbs and slings with which outrageous fortune everlastingly tested him. . . .

When he was a child, his parents set him to learn to read and write, and he developed such a good and clear hand (and I have seen many examples of it) that he could have earned his living by it [as a scribe]. Then he was given over to the study of arithmetic and also of drawing and painting, at which he was talented enough to have become a professional had he so chosen. It was in Pavia that he received his basic schooling in grammar and where he became proficient in Latin . . . And what good stead this must have stood him in when it came to understanding history, both secular and sacred! This was how he spent his earliest years, and this was the foundation on which he would build when he strove to acquire other skills in adolescence and as a young man. And, since the Lord had endowed him with fine judgment, a capacious memory, and a phenomenal appetite for hard work, he consulted many learned men and worked tirelessly at his books and thereby—alongside what I can and do believe to have been a unique capacity granted him for the ministry to which he was destined—he acquired a grasp and mastery of the other fields of learning that would prove vital to his calling: geometry, geography, cosmography, astrology or astronomy, and seamanship.

4

GONZALO FERNÁNDEZ DE OVIEDO

On Columbus's Appearance and Origins

1535–ca. 1549

Gonzalo Fernández de Oviedo (1478–1557) was a royal official and natural historian who spent close to fifty years in the Indies. He was the first to attempt a systematic description of the flora and fauna of the Americas, and his most famous work is the General and Natural History of the Indies *(1535–ca. 1549), which contains information on geography, natural phenomena, anthropology, and history. Oviedo, a tireless champion of the Spanish conquest and occupation of the Americas, constructed an image of a "New World" that was historically dependent upon the Spanish—and in particular on Columbus, the "first discoverer"—but that was by nature unique and autonomous. In this excerpt Oviedo recounts the apocryphal tale of the lost pilot who supposedly told Columbus about lands to the west in the Atlantic.*

Some people say that the New World was known a long time ago and its exact location written down, and all knowledge of it was lost. Then Christopher Columbus, a well-read man and learned in the science of navigation, dared to discover the Indies. Now I do not myself disbelieve this theory, for reasons that will be set forth in the following chapter. However, for contemporaries and posterity I will deal first with the man to whom we owe so much as leader and founder of the great enterprise he began. Christopher Columbus, as I have learned from his compatriots, was born in the province of Liguria, Italy,

Jesús Carrillo, ed., and Diane Avalle-Arce, trans., pref. Anthony Pagden, *Oviedo on Columbus,* Repertorium Columbianum 9 (Turnhout, Belgium: Brepols, 2000), 43–45.

wherein lie the city and dominion of Genoa. Some say he was from Savona, others say from a little village or hamlet called Nervi on the eastern coast two leagues from Genoa; it seems most likely he was from a place called Cogoleto, near Genoa. A decent man of a respectable family, of a good height and appearance, taller than average and strongly built, with a quick eye and regular features. He had red hair, a rather ruddy face and freckles; was well spoken, circumspect, and highly intelligent; a notable Latinist and learned cosmographer; amusing when he wished to be; furious when he was angered.

His ancestors came from Piacenza in Lombardy, on the banks of the river Po. Young Columbus, well-educated and just past adolescence, left his homeland during the life of his father, Domenico. Columbus went east and traveled much, or most, of the Mediterranean, learning the art of navigation by experience. After a few voyages, his spirit rose to wider seas and loftier ideas; he wanted to see the great Ocean Sea, and he went to Portugal. He lived some time in Lisbon in straitened circumstances, but as a grateful son he always sent part of his earnings to his aged father.

The story is told that once a caravel set out from Spain for England with a cargo of wine and foodstuffs and other merchandise the British Isles lack and are accustomed to import. The caravel encountered terrible storms and contrary winds; she ran westward for so many days she fetched up on one or more of the islands of the Indies, landed, and saw naked people like those here. When the winds abated she took on water and firewood. As the story goes, since the ship's cargo was chiefly foodstuffs and wines, the crew was able to survive the hardships of the long voyage and catch a fair wind for Europe. But the return voyage was long and hard, especially for those who in such fear and peril had been forced to sail for four or five months, or even more. Almost all of the crew died on the voyage home, and only the pilot and some three or four of the sailors disembarked in Portugal; these survivors were so ill they also died a short time later.

It is said that the pilot was a close friend of Christopher Columbus's and that he understood something of taking a reading of latitude and had done so for the strange lands he had seen; he told Columbus all this in secret. Columbus begged him to draw a map and mark on it the location of the strange land; Columbus also took the pilot into his house as a friend and got medical attention for him, for he was very ill—but the pilot died like the rest of the sailors. This was how Columbus knew of the Indies and how to get there, and he was the only man in possession of the secret.

5

CHRISTOPHER COLUMBUS

Undated Letter to Fernando and Isabel

1500–1502

In residence in Granada in 1501 after his return from his third voyage to the Indies, Christopher Columbus began to compile a manuscript, eventually referred to by Columbus's son Fernando Colón as the Book of Prophecies. *Designed to be presented to Fernando and Isabel, the manuscript is a collection of biblical, patristic, and philosophical texts whose purpose is to locate the discovery of the Indies—presented as a first step toward the liberation of Jerusalem and the Holy Land from Muslim domination—within the historical schema of the salvation of the human race. Columbus assigns himself a prominent role in these events; in this undated letter to the Catholic rulers, inserted at the beginning of the* Book of Prophecies, *Columbus presents autobiographical and religious themes that demonstrate his suitability for this historical role, reflecting the deepening religiosity of his later years.*

Most Christian and Supreme Rulers: my plan for the restitution of the holy temple to the holy Church Militant is the following:

Most exalted rulers, at a very early age I began sailing the sea and have continued until now. This profession creates a curiosity about the secrets of the world. I have been a sailor for forty years, and I have personally sailed to all the known regions. I have had commerce and conversation with knowledgeable people of the clergy and the laity, Latins and Greeks, Jews and Moors, and with many others of different religions. Our Lord has favored my occupation and has given me an intelligent mind. He has endowed me with a great talent for seamanship; sufficient ability in astrology, geometry, and arithmetic; and the mental and physical dexterity required to draw spherical maps of cities, rivers and mountains, islands and ports, with everything in its proper place.

Roberto Rusconi, ed., and Blair Sullivan, trans., *The 'Book of Prophecies' Edited by Christopher Columbus,* Repertorium Columbianum 3 (Berkeley: University of California Press, 1997), 67–77.

During this time I have studied all kinds of texts: cosmography, histories, chronicles, philosophy, and other disciplines. Through these writings, the hand of Our Lord opened my mind to the possibility of sailing to the Indies and gave me the will to attempt the voyage. With this burning ambition I came to your Highnesses. Everyone who heard about my enterprise rejected it with laughter and ridicule. Neither all the sciences that I mentioned previously nor citations drawn from them were of any help to me. Only Your Highnesses had faith and perseverance. Who could doubt that this flash of understanding was the work of the Holy Spirit, as well as my own? The Holy Spirit illuminated his holy and sacred Scripture, encouraging me in a very strong and clear voice from the forty-four books of the Old Testament, the four evangelists, and twenty-three epistles from the blessed apostles, urging me to proceed. Continually, without ceasing a moment, they insisted that I go on. Our Lord wished to make something clearly miraculous of this voyage to the Indies in order to encourage me and others about the holy temple. I spent seven years here in your royal court discussing the project with many people of great authority and with learned men from all disciplines, and they finally concluded that it was all in vain and abandoned it. But finally, what Jesus Christ Our Redeemer said and had previously said through the mouths of his holy prophets came to be. And so one should believe that the other thing will also happen; and as witness to that, if what has been said is not enough, I offer the holy gospel in which Jesus Christ said that all things would pass away, but not his miraculous word. He also said that everything that had been said by him and written by the prophets must be fulfilled.

I said that I would present my argument for the restitution of the holy temple to the holy Church. I am not relying on my lifetime of navigation and the discussions that I have had with many people from many lands and religions, or on the many disciplines and texts that I spoke of previously. I base what I say only on holy and sacred Scripture, and on the prophetic statements of certain holy persons who through divine revelation have spoken on this subject. Perhaps Your Highnesses and all the others who know me and to whom this letter may be shown will criticize me, publicly or privately, as an uneducated man, an uninformed sailor, an ordinary person, etc. I respond with the words of St. Matthew: "Oh, Lord, how many things you have kept secret from the wise and have made known to the innocent!" [Matt. 11.25] And again from St. Matthew, "As our Lord entered Jerusalem, the children sang, "Hosanna, son of David" [Matt. 21:15–16]. In order to test him, the scribes asked him if he had heard what they were saying; and he answered that he had, saying, "Don't you know that truth comes from the mouths of innocent children" [cf. Ps. 8:3]. Or consider the apostles, who wrote such profound things, in particular St. John, "In the beginning was the Word, and the word was God," etc. [John 1:1]; such great words from uneducated men. I believe that the Holy Spirit operates in Christians, Jews, Moors, and in all others of any religion, not only in the wise, but in the ignorant as well. I met a villager who describes the heavens and the stars and their paths better than others who paid to acquire this knowledge. And I say that the Holy Spirit not only reveals the future to rational creatures, but shows us by means of signs in the heavens and the air and through beasts, however he wishes, and in many other ways too numerous to list and well-known to the entire world.

Holy Scripture attests in the Old Testament, through the mouths of the prophets, and in the New Testament through our redemptor Jesus Christ, that this world will end. The signs of when this must happen are described by Matthew and Mark and Luke, and the prophets frequently predicted the event. St. Augustine[1] said that the world would end in the seventh millennium after its creation [*The City of God,* bk. 22, chap. 30]; the holy theologians agree with him, in particular, the cardinal Pierre d'Ailly[2] in Statement XI and in other passages, as I will indicate below. From the creation of the world or from Adam until the coming of Our Lord Jesus Christ there are 5,343 years and 318 days, according to the calculation made by King Alfonso the Wise, taken to be the most accurate by Pierre d'Ailly in statement X of his *Explanation of the Consistency of Astronomy with Theological and Historical Truth.* Adding to this number 1,500 years, and one not yet completed, gives a total of 6,845 years counted toward the completion of this era. By this count, only 155 years remain of the 7,000 years in which, according to the authorities cited above, the world must come to an end.

Our Redeemer said that before the consummation of this world all that had been written by the prophets would have to be fulfilled [cf. Matt. 24]. The prophets wrote about the future as if it were the past and about the past as if it were yet to happen, and similarly with the present. Sometimes they spoke figuratively, other times more directly, and on occasion quite literally. One says more or less than another or expresses it in a better way. Isaiah is the prophet who is most highly praised by St. Jerome[3] and St. Augustine and the other teachers and is

[1]St. Augustine (354–430) was an early Christian church father and philosopher.
[2]Pierre d'Ailly (1350–1420) was a French cardinal and theologian.
[3]St. Jerome (ca. 342–420) was an early Christian church father and biblical scholar.

appreciated and greatly revered by all. Concerning Isaiah, they say that he was not just a prophet, but also an evangelist; he put all his efforts into describing the future and calling all people to our holy Catholic faith.

Many holy teachers and sacred theologians have written about the prophecies and the other books of holy Scripture. They have greatly enlightened us about things that we did not understand, although they often disagree. Some things are beyond the reach of human intelligence. I repeat my objection to being called presumptuous and uneducated and allege that I am following the wishes of St. Matthew, who said, "Oh Lord, how many things you have kept secret from the wise and have made known to the innocent!" [Matt. 11:25] I offer this on my behalf, along with the benefits of personal experience. Most of the prophecies of holy Scripture have already been fulfilled. The Scriptures say this and the Holy Church loudly and unceasingly is saying it, and no other witness is necessary. I will, however, speak of one prophecy in particular because it bears on my argument and gives me support and happiness whenever I think about it.

I have greatly sinned. Yet, every time that I have asked, I have been protected by the mercy and compassion of Our Lord. I have found the sweetest consolation in throwing off all my cares in order to contemplate his marvelous presence. I have already said that for the voyage to the Indies neither intelligence nor mathematics nor world maps were of any use to me; it was the fulfillment of Isaiah's prophecy. This is what I want to record here in order to remind Your Highnesses and so that you can take pleasure from the things I am going to tell you about Jerusalem on the basis of the same authority. If you have faith in this enterprise, you will certainly have the victory. Your Highnesses, remember the writings of the evangelists and the many promises that Our Redeemer made to us, and the extent to which all this has been tested. When St. Peter stepped into the sea, he was able to walk on its surface, as long as his faith was firm [cf. Matt. 14:28–31]. Whoever has as much faith as a grain of mustard seed will be obeyed by the mountains. Whoever has faith has only to ask for something in order to receive it. Knock and it will be opened to you [cf. Matt. 17:19]. No one should be afraid to undertake any enterprise in the name of Our Savior, as long as it is just and appropriate to his holy service. He helped St. Catherine after testing her.[4] Remember, Your Highnesses, that with very little money you undertook the reconquest of the kingdom of Granada.[5]

---

[4]St. Catherine of Alexandria was martyred in 307 or 310.
[5]Taken after six months of siege on January 2, 1492.

The working out of all things has been left by Our Lord to individual free will, although he advises many. He lacks nothing that the people can give to him. Oh how good is the Lord who wishes the people to do things for which he assumes the responsibility! Day and night and at all times the people should give to him their most devoted thanks.

I said above that much that has been prophesied remains to be fulfilled, and I say that these are the world's great events, and I say that a sign of this is the acceleration of Our Lord's activities in this world. I know this from the recent preaching of the gospel in so many lands. The Calabrian abbot Joachim[6] said that whoever was to rebuild the temple on Mount Zion would come from Spain. The cardinal Pierre d'Ailly wrote at length about the end of the religion of Mohammed and the coming of the Antichrist in his treatise *On the Agreement of Astronomy and History;* he discusses, particularly in the last nine chapters, what many astronomers have said about the ten revolutions of Saturn.

[6]Joachim of Fiore (ca. 1130–1201 or 1202) was an Italian religious of the Cistercian order.

6

CHRISTOPHER COLUMBUS

Letter to Nicolò Oderigo, with "Χρο ferens" Signature
March 21, 1502

Columbus, about to depart for his fourth voyage to the Indies, wrote to Nicolò Oderigo, the Genoese ambassador to Spain, sending him two copies of his "writings," that is, the Book of Privileges *issued to Columbus by Fernando and Isabel, so that they could be kept safely in Genoa. Columbus's signature has been the subject of much scholarly speculation; the only portion that can be deciphered with certainty is the Greek-Latin hybrid version of Columbus's name, Χρο FERENS, "Christ-bearing." It seems to reflect the vision he had formed of himself as the bearer of Christianity to the Americas.*

John Dotson, ed. and trans., and Aldo Agosto, ed., *Christopher Columbus and His Family: The Genoese and Ligurian Documents,* Repertorium Columbianum 4 (Turnhout, Belgium: Brepols, 1998), 171–72.

To the Ambassador Messer Nicolò Oderigo, sir:

The loneliness in which you have left us cannot be described. I have given the book of my writings to Messer Francesco de Rivarolo for him to send it to you with another copy of the letters. I ask you to please write to Sir Diego [Columbus's eldest son] about the pecuniary matters and the place where you put it. Another one will be completed and will be sent to you in the same manner through Messer Francesco. In them you will see new writings. Their majesties promise to give me everything that belongs to me and to put Sir Diego in possession of it all as you will see. I write to Messer Juan Luis and to Madonna Catalina. The letter is enclosed with this one. I am about to leave in the name of the Holy Trinity with the first good weather with a large crew. May the Lord keep you. Done 21 March 1502 in Seville. At your command

.S.

.S. A .S.

X M Y

Χρο FERENS[1]

[1]The first three lines of this signature have not been definitely deciphered.

7

BARTOLOMÉ DE LAS CASAS

On Columbus as an Instrument of God's Will

ca. 1527–1563

Documents 7, 8, and 9 offer assessments of Columbus by his contemporaries. At the beginning of the section of his History *devoted to Columbus, Las Casas specifically describes him as the man chosen by God to bring knowledge of the Christian religion to the peoples of the Americas.*

Nigel Griffin, ed. and trans., intro. Anthony Pagden, *Las Casas on Columbus: Background and the Second and Fourth Voyages,* Repertorium Columbianum 7 (Turnhout, Belgium: Brepols, 1999), 23.

In which it is shown that the discovery of these Indies was a marvelous event fashioned by God. And how it would seem that Divine Providence chose for this purpose the admiral who discovered them, for Providence customarily endows those it selects for a particular task with the necessary virtues and qualities. Of the land of birth, lineage, origins, forebears, first name and family name, person, appearance, behavior, character, customs, speech, conversation, religion, and Christian faith of Christopher Columbus. . . .

8

GONZALO FERNÁNDEZ DE OVIEDO

On Columbus as "First Discoverer"

1535–ca. 1549

Oviedo placed Columbus—as a heroic figure of Spanish history and "first discoverer"—at the starting point of the process of Spanish imperial expansion, the description of which was the central project of his General and Natural History of the Indies.

No writer ever knew about most of the animals living in those parts, including the ones I mention here, since they are in a region and a land which was unknown until our times and was not mentioned either in Ptolemy's cosmography or any other until the admiral Christopher Columbus made it known to us. Surely this deed is more worthy and without possible comparison, a bigger achievement than Hercules's having opened the Mediterranean Sea to the ocean, because before him, the Greeks did not know about this opening. . . . It is certain that if Columbus had lived in their times, the ancients would have thought that a gold statue of him was insufficient payment.

. . .

Jesús Carrillo, ed., and Diane Avalle-Arce, trans., *Oviedo on Columbus,* Repertorium Columbianum 9 (Turnhout, Belgium: Brepols, 2000), 40, 90.

My conscience incites me to begin this second volume of the history (concerning Tierra Firme) with Christopher Columbus, the discoverer, author, and founder of exploration in the Indies, islands and Tierra Firme of the Ocean Sea. This praise and glory is his and his alone. But chronology requires me to begin with Captain Ferdinand Magellan, who discovered the great and famous strait to the south of Tierra Firme. . . . In order not to leave out the admiral or anyone else, so no one can complain of me, I will relate punctually what captains and private persons followed the laudable discoverer, and when and what discoveries each one made. So the admiral keeps the preeminence and superiority of first discoverer of undying memory, and the rest receive their due.

9

AGOSTINO GIUSTINIANI, PSALTER

On Columbus the Evangelist

1516

Agostino Giustiniani (1479–1536), a Genoese prelate and scholar, was an authority on Eastern studies and in 1517 became the first professor of Hebrew at the University of Paris. In 1516 he published a polyglot or multiple-language Bible (Hebrew, Latin, Greek, Arabic, and Aramaic), the first in Europe.

"And their words went out unto the ends of the earth" [Ps. 19:4]: at least in our times, when practically another world has been discovered and added to the assembly of Christians by the remarkable feat of daring of the Genoese Christopher Columbus. Indeed, since Columbus himself often predicted that he had been chosen by God so that this prophecy might be fulfilled by him, I have judged that it is not inappropriate to insert an account of his life here. It was Christopher, then,

Geoffrey Symcox and Luciano Formisano, eds., Theodore J. Cachey Jr. and John C. McLucas, trans., *Italian Reports on America 1493–1522: Accounts by Contemporary Observers,* Repertorium Columbianum 12 (Turnhout, Belgium: Brepols, 2002), 77–80.

whose family name was Columbus, Genoese by nationality, of humble stock, who in our time and by his own industry, explored more lands and seas in a few months than virtually all other mortals in all the preceding centuries: it is an amazing thing, but has been proved and certified not only by the witness of many ships, but indeed by that of whole fleets and armies of men who have traveled there and back.

.   .   .

After the completion of his remarkable voyages, Columbus returned to Spain and fulfilled the obligation of what he had said. . . . When Columbus himself died, he did not forget his dear homeland, but left the tenth part of all the revenues he possessed to the bank which is called St. George's, and which the Genoese consider their show-piece, the ornament and support of the whole republic. Such was the end of this very famous man; if he had been born in the time of the Greek heroes, he would doubtless have been made one of the gods.

2

The Four Voyages

First Voyage, 1492–1493

10

Santa Fe Capitulations

Santa Fe, April 17, 1492

After Fernando and Isabel conquered Granada in January 1492, they agreed to Columbus's proposal to sail west toward Asia on a commercial and exploratory voyage. On April 17, 1492, in the town of Santa Fe de Granada they drew up a memorandum of intent to form a business partnership with Columbus; this royal commitment to Columbus is known as the Santa Fe Capitulations. Fernando and Isabel promised Columbus five major concessions: commission as admiral; commission as viceroy and governor general; right to one-tenth of all gold, precious stones, and merchandise the monarchs acquired from his admiralty; jurisdiction over lawsuits arising from commerce in his admiralty; and the right to invest up to one-eighth of the costs of all vessels outfitted for commerce in his admiralty and to keep up to one-eighth of the profits.

The things requested and that Your Highnesses give and grant to Sir Christopher Columbus in partial reward for what he will discover on the voyage that now, with the help of God, he is to make on the Ocean Seas in the service of Your Highnesses, are the following:

Helen Nader, ed. and trans., Luciano Formisano, ed., *The Book of Privileges Issued to Christopher Columbus by King Fernando and Queen Isabel 1492–1502,* Repertorium Columbianum 2 (Berkeley: University of California Press, 1996), 63–66.

First, Your Highnesses, as the lords you are of the Ocean Seas, appoint Sir Christopher Columbus from now on as your admiral on all those islands and mainland[1] discovered or acquired by his command and expertise in the Ocean Seas during his lifetime and, after his death, by his heirs and successors one after the other in perpetuity, with privileges and prerogatives equal to those that Sir Alfonso Enríquez, your high admiral of Castile, and his other predecessors in the office held in their districts.[2]

It pleases Their Highnesses. Juan de Coloma.[3]

Also, Your Highnesses appoint Sir Christopher your viceroy and governor general in all those islands and any mainland and islands that he may discover and acquire in the seas. For the governance of each and every one of them, he will nominate three persons for each office, and Your Highnesses will select and appoint the one most beneficial to your service, and thus the lands that our Lord permits him to find and acquire will be best governed to the service of Your Highnesses.

It pleases Their Highnesses. Juan de Coloma.

You wish him to have and take for himself one-tenth of all and any merchandise, whether pearls, precious stones, gold, silver, spices, and any other things and merchandise of whatever kind, name, or sort it may be, that is bought, exchanged, found, acquired, and obtained within the limits of the admiralty that Your Highnesses from now on bestow on Sir Christopher, deducting all the relevant expenses incurred, so that, of what remains clear and free, he may take and keep one-tenth for himself and do with it as he pleases, reserving the other nine-tenths for Your Highnesses.

It pleases Their Highnesses. Juan de Coloma.

Should any lawsuits arise on account of the merchandise that he brings back from the islands and mainland acquired or discovered, or over merchandise taken in exchange from other merchants there in the place where this commerce and trade is held and done, and if taking cognizance of such suits belongs to him by virtue of the privileges pertaining to his office of admiral, may it please Your Highnesses that

---

[1]When Fernando and Isabel used the term *mainland,* they were hoping that Columbus would be able to establish Castilian sovereignty on some portion of the Asian coast.

[2]In 1405 King Enrique III of Castile had granted the admiralty of Castile to Alfonso Enríquez as a hereditary office. This provided the legal precedent that Columbus sought for the heritability of his own office as admiral of the Ocean Sea.

[3]Juan de Coloma (d. 1517) was secretary to Fernando of Aragón throughout his reign (1479–1516).

he or his deputy, and no other judge, shall be authorized to take cognizance of and give judgment on it from now on.

It pleases Their Highnesses, if it pertains to the office of admiral and conforms to what the admiral Sir Alfonso Enríquez and his other predecessors had in their districts, and if it be just. Juan de Coloma.

On all vessels outfitted for trade and business, each time, whenever, and as often as they are outfitted, Sir Christopher Columbus, if he wishes, may contribute and pay one-eighth of all that is spent on the outfitting and likewise he may have and take one-eighth of the profits that result from such outfitting.

It pleases Their Highnesses. Juan de Coloma.

These are authorized and dispatched with the replies from Your Highnesses at the end of each article. In the town of Santa Fe de La Vega de Granada, on the seventeenth day of April in the year of the birth of our savior Jesus Christ one thousand four hundred and ninety-two.

I, the King I; I, the Queen. By command of the king and queen. Juan de Coloma.

11

Granada Capitulations

Granada, April 30, 1492

In Granada on April 30, 1492, Fernando and Isabel issued a writ appointing Columbus to the royal offices he had requested, a document known as the Granada Capitulations. The monarchs agreed that Columbus would be their hereditary admiral of the Ocean Sea, and they appointed him viceroy and governor of any islands or mainland he might discover and take possession of in the name of the Spanish monarchs.

Sir Fernando and Lady Isabel, by the grace of God king and queen of Castile, León, Aragón, Sicily, Granada, Toledo, Valencia, Galicia, the

Helen Nader, ed. and trans., Luciano Formisano, ed., *The Book of Privileges Issued to Christopher Columbus by King Fernando and Queen Isabel 1492–1502,* Repertorium Columbianum 2 (Berkeley: University of California Press, 1996), 66–69.

Balearics, Seville, Sardinia, Córdoba, Corsica, Murcia, Jaén, the Algarve, Algeçiras, Gibraltar and the Canary Islands, count and countess of Barcelona, lords of Vizcaya and Molina, dukes of Athens and Neopatria, counts of Roussillon and Cerdagne, marquises of Oristano and Goceano.

Because you, Christopher Columbus, are going at our command with some of our ships and personnel to discover and acquire certain islands and mainland in the Ocean Sea, and it is hoped that, with the help of God, some of the islands and mainland in the Ocean Sea will be discovered and acquired by your command and expertise, it is just and reasonable that you should be remunerated for placing yourself in danger for our service.

Wanting to honor and bestow favor for these reasons, it is our grace and wish that you, Christopher Columbus, after having discovered and acquired these islands and mainland in the Ocean Sea, will be our admiral of the islands and mainland that you discover and acquire and will be our admiral, viceroy, and governor of them. You will be empowered from that time forward to call yourself Sir Christopher Columbus, and thus your sons and successors in this office and post may entitle themselves sir, admiral, viceroy, and governor of them.

You and your proxies will have the authority to exercise the office of admiral together with the offices of viceroy and governor of the islands and mainland that you discover and acquire. You will have the power to hear and dispose of all the lawsuits and cases, civil and criminal, related to the offices of admiral, viceroy, and governor, as you determine according to the law, and as the admirals of our kingdoms are accustomed to administer it. You and your proxies will have the power to punish and penalize delinquents as well as exercising the offices of admiral, viceroy, and governor in all matters pertaining to these offices. You will enjoy and benefit from the fees and salaries attached, belonging, and corresponding to these offices, just as our high admiral enjoys and is accustomed to them in the admiralty of our kingdoms.

With this our writ or its transcript certified by a public clerk, we order Prince Sir Juan, our most dear and very beloved son, and the princes, dukes, prelates, marquises, counts, masters, priors, and commanders of the orders; royal councilors, judges of our appellate court, and judges and any other justices of our household, court, and chancery; subcommanders and commanders of our castles, forts, and buildings; all municipal councils, royal judges, corregidors, municipal judges, sheriffs, appeals judges, councilmen, parish delegates, commissioned and noncommissioned officers, municipal officials, and voting citizens of all the cities, towns, and villages of these our kingdoms and domains and of those that you may conquer and acquire; captains, masters, mates, warrant officers, sailors and ship's crews; and each and every one of our subjects and citizens now and in the future, that, having discovered and acquired any islands and mainland in the Ocean Sea, once you or your designated representative have performed the oath and formalities required in such cases, from then on you shall be accepted and regarded for the rest of your life, and your sons and successors after you for evermore, as our admiral of the Ocean Sea and viceroy and governor of the islands and mainland that you, Sir Christopher Columbus, discover and acquire.

All these officials and people shall put into effect everything pertaining to these offices, together with you and the proxies you appoint to the offices of admiral, viceroy, and governor. They shall pay and cause to be paid to you the salary, fees, and other perquisites of these offices. They shall observe and cause to be observed for you all the honors, gifts, favors, liberties, privileges, prerogatives, exemptions, immunities, and each and all of the other things that, by virtue of the offices of admiral, viceroy, and governor, you should receive and that should be paid to you fully and completely, in such a way that nothing will be withheld from you. They shall not place or consent to place hindrance or obstacle against you in any way.

For with this writ we grant to you from now on the offices of admiral, viceroy, and governor as a hereditary right for evermore, and we grant you actual and prospective possession of them, as well as the authority to administer them and collect the dues and salaries attached and pertaining to each of them.

If it should be necessary for you, and you should request it of them, we command our chancellor, notaries, and other officials who preside over the table with our seals to give, issue, forward, and seal our letter of privilege with the circle of signatures, in the strongest, firmest, and most sufficient manner that you may request and find necessary. None of you or them shall do otherwise in any way concerning this, under penalty of our displeasure and a fine of 10,000 *maravedís*[1] for our treasury on each person who does the contrary.

Furthermore, we command the man who shows you this writ to summon you to appear before us in our court, wherever we may be, within fifteen days of having been cited, under the same penalty.

---

[1]In Christian Spain a *maravedí* was a unit of accounting, not a circulating coin; 375 *maravedís* were the equivalent of a Venetian gold ducat.

Under this same penalty, we command every public clerk who may be summoned for this purpose to give the person showing this writ to him a certificate to that effect, inscribed with his rubric, so that we may know how well our command is obeyed.

Given in our city of Granada on the thirtieth day of the month of April in the year of the birth of our Lord Jesus Christ one thousand four hundred and ninety-two. I, the King; I, the Queen. I, Juan de Coloma, secretary of the king and queen our lords, had this written at their command.

12

CHRISTOPHER COLUMBUS

Selected Entries from the Log

August 3, 1492–March 15, 1493

Only one written record of his four voyages to the Indies kept by Christopher Columbus has survived: a text known as Columbus's Log, a daily account of the first voyage beginning with the departure from Palos in August 1492 and concluding with the return seven months later. The original Log in Columbus's handwriting has been lost, but a copy in the handwriting of Bartolomé de Las Casas exists. Las Casas, who apparently saw the original source, reproduced a version of Columbus's Log, sometimes directly quoting Columbus's entries (using phrases such as "these are his very words") and sometimes paraphrasing them. The degree to which Las Casas's paraphrases depart from the original source is not known.

Prologue addressed by Christopher Columbus to the king and queen of Spain:

In the name of our Lord Jesus Christ. Because, O most Christian, most elevated, most excellent, and most powerful princes, king and

Francesca Lardicci, ed., Cynthia L. Chamberlin and Blair Sullivan, trans., *A Synoptic Edition of the Log of Columbus's First Voyage,* Repertorium Columbianum 6 (Turnhout, Belgium: Brepols, 1999), 37–136.

queen of the Spains and of the islands of the sea, our lords, in this present year of 1492, after Your Highnesses had put an end to the war with the Muslims, who had been reigning in Europe, and finished the war in the great city of Granada, where on January 2 in this same year I saw the royal standards of Your Highnesses raised by force of arms atop the towers of the Alhambra, which is the fortress of that city, and I saw the Muslim king come out to the gates of the city and kiss the royal hands of Your Highnesses and of my lord the crown prince; and later in the same month, based upon the information that I had given to Your Highnesses about the lands of India and about a prince who is called the Grand Khan (which in our vernacular tongue means "king of kings") — that many times he and his predecessors had sent to Rome to request teachers of our holy faith who might instruct him in it, but that the Holy Father [the pope] never had provided him with this and so many peoples had been lost, falling into idolatries and adopting for themselves damnable sects — Your Highnesses, as Catholic Christians and princes who love the holy Christian faith, exalters of it and enemies of the sect of Mohammed and of all idolatries and heresies, thought to send me, Christopher Columbus, to those abovementioned regions of India to see the princes, peoples, and lands, and their disposition and all the rest, and determine what method should be undertaken for their conversion to our holy faith; and you ordered that I not go by land to the Orient, the customary route, but instead by a western route, where we do not know with certainty to this day that anyone has gone. So it was that, after having expelled all the Jews from your kingdoms and domains, in that same month of January, Your Highnesses commanded that I should go to the said regions of India with a suitable fleet; and for this reason you bestowed great favors upon me and ennobled me, so that from that moment on I might call myself "sir" and be the lord high admiral of the Ocean Sea, and my eldest son should succeed me in like manner, and his descendants him likewise, generation after generation, forever and ever. I departed from the city of Granada on May 12 of that same year 1492, a Saturday, and arrived at the town of Palos, which is a seaport, where I fitted out three vessels amply suited for such an endeavor. I departed from this port well-stocked with supplies and with many seamen on August 3 of that same year, a Friday, half an hour before sunrise. I set out for Your Highnesses' Canary Islands, which are in the Ocean Sea, in order to begin my journey from there and sail until I should arrive in the Indies, there to deliver Your Highnesses' embassy to those princes and fulfill what you had ordered me to do in this respect. And for this reason, I have thought to write down this entire voyage very precisely, everything which I may do and see and experience, day by day, as will be seen from now on. In addition, my lords and princes, to writing down every night what has happened during the day, and in the day what distance I have sailed during the night, I have it in mind to draw a new nautical chart on which I will locate the sea and the lands of the Ocean Sea in their proper places, each beneath its wind, and moreover to write a book and put the likeness of everything in it in drawings, in their equinoctial latitudes and their longitudes from the west. It is above all important that I forget about sleep and pay great attention to navigation, for in this way duty is fulfilled; and these things will be hard work.

Friday, August 3[1]
We departed on Friday, the third day of August in the year 1492, from the Saltés bar at eight o'clock. We traveled south, with a strong breeze until the setting of the sun, sixty miles, which is fifteen leagues; afterwards, southwest and south, a quarter southwest, which was the route to the Canaries.[2]

Thursday, October 11
The admiral sailed west-southwest; they took on a lot of water, more than they had taken on during the whole voyage. They saw some terns and a green reed near the ship. The crew of the caravel *Pinta* saw a cane and a stick, and they took up another small stick that had been worked, it appeared, with iron, a piece of cane and another plant that grows on land, and a small board. The crew of the caravel *Niña* also saw other signs of land and a small branch loaded with reddish fruit. At these signs they breathed more easily, and everyone cheered up. This day they traveled, until the sun had set, twenty-seven leagues.

After the sun had set, the admiral sailed his original course west; they would travel twelve miles an hour, and until two hours after midnight they would travel ninety miles, which is twenty-two and a half leagues. Because the caravel *Pinta* was a swifter sailer and was going out ahead of the admiral, she found land and made the signals that the admiral had ordered. A sailor who was named Rodrigo de Triana saw this land first, although the admiral, at ten o'clock at night standing in

---

[1] In 1492 the Julian calendar was in effect; thus the dates given by Columbus are ten days earlier than the corresponding dates on the Gregorian calendar that we use today.

[2] The Roman mile used by Columbus was equal to 1,480 meters and the league was equal to four Roman miles. Columbus set sail from the Canaries heading west on September 9.

the sterncastle, saw a light, but it was so overcast that he did not want to claim that it might be land. But he called Pedro Gutiérrez, a keeper of the king's dais, and told him that there seemed to be a light and he should have a look; and so he did, and saw it. The admiral also told this to Rodrigo Sánchez de Segovia, whom the king and queen had sent in the fleet as inspector, who saw nothing because he was not in a place where he could see it. After the admiral had spoken of it, it was seen once or twice again; it was like a little wax candle that was being raised and lifted, which seemed to few to be an indication of land. But the admiral was certain that he was close to land. Thus, when they recited the *Salve*[3]—which all sailors are accustomed to recite and sing together in their own way, and all are present—he entreated and exhorted them to keep a sharp lookout from the forecastle and to watch carefully for land and said that he would give a silk doublet to the first person who sighted land, not to mention the other grants that the monarchs had promised—10,000 *maravedís* in perpetuity to whoever would see it first. Two hours after midnight, land appeared; they were probably about two leagues away from it. They took in the sails and were left with the main course, which is the mainsail without bonnets, and heaved to, biding their time until morning on Friday, when they reached a small island of the Lucayos which was called Guanahaní in the language of the Indians.

Soon they saw naked people; and the admiral went ashore in an armed boat, along with Martín Alonso Pinzón and Vicente Yáñez, his brother, who was the captain of the *Niña*. The admiral took up the royal banner, and the captains two banners with the green cross which the admiral carried on all the vessels as a standard, bearing an F and a Y,[4] and above each letter its crown, one at one end of the ✠ and the other at the other end [see Figure 5]. Once they were on shore, they saw very green trees, lots of water, and different kinds of fruit. The admiral called his two captains and the rest of the crew who had come ashore, Rodrigo de Escobedo, secretary of the whole fleet, and Rodrigo Sánchez de Segovia, and told them to give their faith and witness to the fact that he, in the presence of everyone, was taking, and in fact had taken, possession of that island for his lords the king and queen, making the declarations that were required, which are contained more fully in the testimonials that were made there in writing. Soon many people of the island gathered at that place. . . .

---

[3]The *Salve Regina*, a hymn in honor of the Virgin Mary.
[4]"F" and "Y" were the initials of the Spanish monarchs, Fernando and Ysabel, or Isabel.

Figure 5. *The Indians of Guanahaní Greet Columbus.*

In this detailed German engraving, made about one hundred years after Columbus's first voyage, the Taínos are given European physical characteristics; furthermore, the jewels that they are offering to Columbus and his men resemble those of the Italian Renaissance. The raising of the cross evokes the evangelical justification for Columbus's enterprise of the Indies.

Source: From Theodor de Bry, *America*, part 4, plate 9, Frankfurt 1594.

SATURDAY, OCTOBER 13

As soon as dawn came, many of these people came to the beach, all of them young, as I have said, and all of good stature, a very beautiful people. Their hair is not curly, but thick and flowing like a horse's mane, and they all have very broad foreheads and heads, more so than any other race that I have seen so far. Their eyes are very beautiful and not small; and none of them are dark, but rather the color of Canary Islanders, nor should one expect anything else, since this island is in the same latitude as the island of Hierro in the Canary Islands. All of them, in general, have very straight legs, and they have no bellies, except very trim ones. They came to the ship in *almadías,* which are canoes made from tree trunks in the shape of a long boat, all of one piece and marvelously crafted according to the fashion of this land. There are large ones in which forty to forty-five people came, and other smaller ones, down to some in which only a single person came. They row with a paddle like a baker's shovel and go along marvelously. If it capsizes, they immediately throw themselves into the water to swim and right it and bail it out with gourds that they bring along. They brought balls of spun cotton, parrots, javelins, and other little things that it would be tedious to write down; and they gave it all for whatever might be given to them. I was attentive and attempted to learn if they had gold, and I saw that some of them were wearing a little piece hung through a hole that they have in their noses. Using gestures, I was able to learn that if one went south or circled the island to the south, there was a king there who had large vessels of gold and had a lot of it. I attempted to get them to go there, but then saw that they did not know the way there. I decided to wait until the next day in the afternoon and then depart for the southwest, for, as many of them showed me, they said that there was land to the south and to the southwest and to the northwest, and that these peoples from the northwest often came to fight them. So I will go southwest to look for gold and precious stones. This island is very big and very low-lying, with very green trees, lots of water, and a very large lake in the middle, without a single mountain, and all of it is so green that it is a pleasure to look at it. These people are very gentle, and because of their desire to have some of our things, and believing that nothing is to be given to them unless they give something, but because they do not have anything, they take what they can and then jump into the water to swim away. Moreover, everything that they have, they give for anything that may be given them, for they traded even for pieces of ceramic bowls and broken glass cups, to the point that I even saw them give sixteen balls of spun cotton for three Portuguese *ceutís,*[5] which are worth one Castilian *blanca,*[6] and in the balls there would be more than an *arroba*[7] of spun cotton. I should have prohibited this and not let anyone take any of it, except that I had commanded that all of it be taken for Your Highnesses, if it existed in quantity. Cotton grows here on this island, but because of the short time, I could not be completely sure. The gold that they wear hung in their noses originates here also; but so as not to waste time, I want to go and see if I can come upon the island of Cipangu.[8] Now, since it was night, all the Indians went ashore in their *almadías.* . . .

SUNDAY, OCTOBER 28

The admiral went south-southwest from there in search of the nearest part of the island of Cuba and went up a very beautiful river, very free from the danger of shallows or other obstacles; all the coast that he traveled along thereabouts was very deep and very clear up to the shore. The river's mouth was twelve fathoms deep and was wide enough for tacking; he anchored inside, he says, the length of a cannon shot. The admiral says that he never saw such a beautiful thing, all full of trees near the river, beautiful and green and unlike our own, with flowers and fruit, each one after its own kind, and many large and small birds that sang very sweetly. There was a large number of palm trees of a different kind from those of Guinea and from our own, of a middling height, their trunks without bark, but very large leaves with which the natives cover their buildings. The land was very flat. The admiral got into the boat and went ashore and arrived at two buildings that he believed to belong to fishermen who had fled out of fear. In one of them he found a dog that never barked; and in both buildings he found nets of palm twine, little cords, fishhooks of horn, fish spears made of bone, and other fishing gear, and many hearths inside; he believed that many people came together in each house. He commanded that nothing in all of it be touched, and so it was done. The grass was high, as it is in Andalucía in April and May; he found a lot of purslane and blite. He returned to the boat and went up the river for quite a while; it was, he says, a great pleasure to see that greenery, those woods, and the birds, so that he could not leave them to go back.

---

[5]A *ceutí* was a Portuguese coin; 3 *ceutís* equaled 1 *blanca.*
[6]A *blanca* was a small copper coin.
[7]An *arroba* was a unit of weight equal to 11.5 kilograms.
[8]Cipangu was the Chinese name for Japan, used by Marco Polo (1254–1324) in *Il milione,* the story of his travels.

He says that that island is the most beautiful that eyes have seen, full of very good harbors and deep rivers; and a sea that seems that it must never rise, for the grass on the beach almost reached to the water, which it usually does not do where the sea is rough. Until then he never had felt that the sea might be rough in all those islands. The island, he says, is full of very beautiful mountains; although they are not very great in length, they are high, and all of the rest of the land is high, like Sicily. It is full of many sources of water, according to what he could understand from the Indians whom he is bringing with him, whom he took on the island of Guanahaní, who tell him by means of signs that there are ten large rivers and that in their canoes they cannot circle the island in twenty days. While he was going towards the shore with the vessels, two *almadías,* or canoes, came out; and when they saw that the sailors were getting into the boat and were rowing to go look at the river's depth to learn where they were to anchor, the canoes fled. The Indians had said that there were gold mines and pearls on the island, and the admiral saw a place suited for the latter and for clams, which are a sign of pearls. The admiral understood that large ships belonging to the Grand Khan came there and that it was ten days' journey from there to the mainland. The admiral named that river and port after San Salvador. . . .

THURSDAY, NOVEMBER 1

As the sun was rising, the admiral sent the boats ashore to the buildings that were there, and they found that all the people had fled. After quite some time a man appeared, and the admiral commanded them to let him be reassured, and the boats returned. After he had eaten, the admiral again sent ashore one of the Indians he was carrying, who shouted to the man from afar, saying that the natives should not be afraid for the Christians were good people and did no harm to anyone, and they were not from the Grand Khan; on the contrary, they had given away some of their property on many islands where they had been. The Indian jumped in to swim and went ashore, and two of the people from that place took him by the arms and brought him to a building where they questioned him. Once they were certain that he was not going to do them harm, they were reassured; and then more than sixteen *almadías,* or canoes, came up to the ships with spun cotton and other little things of theirs, of which the admiral commanded that nothing be taken so that the natives might know that the admiral was not looking for anything but gold, which they call *nuçay.* So during the entire day they came and went from the shore to the ships, and some of the Christians went ashore very safely. The admiral saw no gold on any of them, but he says that he saw on one of them a piece of wrought silver hanging from his nose, which he took as a sign that there was silver in that land. The Indians said by means of gestures that before three days passed, many merchants from inland would come from inland to purchase some of the things that the Christians bring there, and they would give news of the king of that land, who, according to what could be understood from the gestures they made, was four days' journey from there, for they had sent many men throughout the land to let him know about the admiral. "These people," says the admiral, "are of the same nature and customs as the others found so far, with no religion that I may recognize, for so far I have not seen those whom I bring with me make any prayer, but they do say the *Salve* and the *Ave Maria*[9] with their hands lifted to the sky as they are shown and make the sign of the cross. Their whole language is the same as well, and they are all friends; and I believe that all these may be islands, and that they are at war with the Grand Khan, whom they call Cavila, and their province Bafán. They also go around naked, like the others." This is what the admiral says. The river, he says, is very deep, and at its mouth vessels can come alongside the shore. The fresh water does not come within a league of the mouth, but it is very fresh. "It is certain," the admiral says, "that this is the mainland, and that I am," he says, "off Zayton or Quisay,[10] a hundred leagues, a little more or less, from one or the other; and this is clearly demonstrated by the sea, which comes on in a different condition than it has come on until now, and yesterday, when I was going northwest, I found that it was cold."

FRIDAY, NOVEMBER 2
The admiral decided to send two Spaniards; one was called Rodrigo de Jerez, who used to live in Ayamonte, and the other was a certain Luis de Torres, who had lived with the governor of Murcia and had been a Jew and knew, the admiral says, Hebrew, Chaldean, and even a bit of Arabic. The admiral sent two Indians with these men, one of those whom he had brought with him from Guanahaní and a second from those buildings that were settled at the river. He gave them strands of beads with which to buy something to eat if they should need it and a period of six days within which they should return. He gave them samples of spices, to see if they might come upon any of them. He gave them instructions as to how they were to ask about the

---

[9]A prayer in honor of the Virgin Mary.
[10]Zayton and Quisay were Chinese cities described by Marco Polo.

king of that land and what they were to say on behalf of the monarchs of Castile and how they had sent the admiral to deliver their letters and a gift on their behalf. They were to learn about his situation, establish friendship with him, and favor him in whatever he might have need of from them, etc.; and they should learn about certain provinces, harbors, and rivers that the admiral had had news about and how far they were from there, etc. Here, this night, the admiral took his latitude with a quadrant and found that he was forty-two degrees from the equator. He says that, according to his count, he had traveled 1,142 leagues from the island of Hierro, and he still asserts that this is the mainland. . . .

FRIDAY, NOVEMBER 23
The admiral sailed all day toward the land to the south, always with little wind, but the current never let him reach it; on the contrary, today he was as far from it at the setting of the sun as he had been in the morning. The wind was east-northeasterly and favorable for going south, except that it was light. Above this cape another shore, or cape, projected, which also goes east, which the Indians whom he was bringing called *bohío*.[11] They said it was very large and that there were people upon it who had one eye in the middle of their foreheads and others whom they called Cannibals, of whom they showed themselves to have a great fear. Once they saw that he follows this course, he says, they could not speak, for those people used to eat them and are very well-armed. The admiral says that indeed he believes that there was something in it, but that, since they were armed, they would be a rational people. He believed that these Cannibals had taken some of them captive, and that, because the captives had not returned to their own lands, they said that they had been eaten by them. They believed the same thing about the Christians and the admiral, when some of them first saw them. . . .

TUESDAY, DECEMBER 25
On the previous day, while sailing with little wind from the Mar de Santo Tomé toward the Punta Santa[12]—he stayed a league off the point until the first watch was over, which would be at eleven o'clock at night—the admiral decided to lie down to sleep, because it had

---

[11]The Tainos used the word *bohío,* "house," to indicate the island on which they lived.

[12]Columbus was sailing along the northern coast of Hispaniola, off what is now Haiti.

been two days and a night since he had slept. Since it was calm, the sailor who had been steering the ship decided to go to sleep as well and left the helm to a ship's boy, although the admiral had always strictly forbidden throughout the voyage—whether there were wind or calm, it should be known—that the ship's boys be allowed to steer. The admiral had been safe from sandbars and rocks, for on Sunday they had passed a good three and a half leagues to the east of that Punta Santa, and the sailors had seen the entire coast and the shoals that are there from that Punta Santa for a good three leagues to the east-southeast, and they saw where one could pass through these. He had not done that before during this entire voyage. Our Lord desired that, at twelve o'clock at night—since they had seen the admiral go to bed to rest and they had seen that it was dead calm and that the sea was as calm as water in a large bowl—the crew all lay down to sleep and the tiller was left in the hand of that boy. And the currents carried the ship onto one of those sand banks, which, even though it was night, were making a noise so that they might be heard and seen a good league off; but she went up on it so gently that it barely was felt. The boy, who felt the rudder touch and heard the sound of the sea, called out, at which the admiral came up; but it happened so fast that no one else even had felt that they were aground. Then the ship's master, whose watch it was, came out. The admiral told him and the other crewmen to heave out the launch they were carrying astern and to take an anchor and cast it astern. The master, along with many others, jumped into the launch, and the admiral thought that they were doing what he had commanded them; but they did not care about anything but fleeing to the caravel, which was half a league to windward. The caravel, acting virtuously, would not receive them, and for this reason they went back to the ship; but the caravel's boat was there first. When the admiral saw that they were running away—and that it was ebb tide (which means that the water was decreasing, or that it was running down) and the waters still were ebbing, and that the ship already lay beam-on to the sea—seeing no other remedy, he commanded that the mast be struck down and the ship lightened of as much as they could, to see if they could get her off. But as the waters were dropping, she could not be set to rights, and she listed beam-on into the sea, even though the sea was low or nothing, and then the planking seams opened up. The admiral went to the caravel in order to place the ship's crew in safety aboard the caravel; and since a light wind already was blowing from the land, and moreover much of the night still remained and they did not know how far the sand banks stretched, he passed the time hove-to until it was day. Later he went out to the ship from within the sand-bank shoal. First he sent the launch ashore with Diego de Arana of Córdoba, lieutenant-commander of the fleet, and Pedro Gutiérrez, comptroller of the royal household, to inform the king,[13] who, on Saturday, had invited him to visit and begged him to come with the vessels to his harbor. He had his town further inland, a league and a half's journey from that sand bank. They say that the king, when he learned of it, wept and sent all his people from the village with many very large canoes to unload everything from the ship. Thus it was done, and in a very short time everything was unloaded from the decks; such was the great assistance and rapidity that that king gave to the task. And the king, in person, and his brothers and relatives were showing as much diligence, both aboard the ship and in keeping safe what had been brought ashore, so that everything might be in very safe keeping. From time to time he sent one of his relatives, weeping, to the admiral, to console him, telling him not to be distressed or angry, for he would give him everything he might have. The admiral assures the monarchs that in no part of Castile could such good care have been taken of all their things, so that not even a lacing was missing. The king commanded everything to be placed near the buildings; in the meantime, some buildings were being emptied that he wanted to give to the admiral, where everything might be placed and kept. He commanded that armed men be placed around everything, who should keep watch all night. "He and all the people were weeping," says the admiral. "They are such loving people, without greed and amenable in everything, that I assure Your Highnesses that I believe there is no better people, or better land, in the world. They love their neighbors as themselves, and they have the sweetest way of speaking in the world: gentle and always with a smile. They go about naked, men and women, just as their mothers bore them, but Your Highnesses may believe that among themselves they have very good customs; and the king has a wonderful stateliness, so composed in a certain fashion that it is a pleasure to see it all. They have wonderful memories, and they want to see everything, and they ask what something is and what it is for." The admiral says all this just in this way.

WEDNESDAY, DECEMBER 26
Today at sunrise the king [Guacanagarí] of that land, who was in that village, came to the caravel *Niña,* where the admiral was and, almost

---

[13]The Taino chief, or cacique, Guacanagarí.

weeping, told the admiral that he should not be distressed, that he would give him everything he had and that he had given to the Christians who were on shore two very large buildings and would give them more if they had need, and as many canoes as could load and unload the ship and put the cargo ashore, and as many people as the admiral might want. He said that he had had it done so yesterday, so that no one had taken a scrap of bread or any other thing whatsoever. "So faithful and without covetousness of another's property are they," says the admiral, "and so was that virtuous king, above all the others." While the admiral was talking with the king, another canoe came from another place, which was carrying some pieces of gold, which the native wanted to give in exchange for a bell; for they desired nothing else so much as bells, for the canoe did not even arrive alongside before the natives were calling out and displaying the pieces of gold, saying *"Chuq chuque,"* for "bells," for they are on the point of going crazy for them. After this had been seen, and when these canoes that were from other places were going away, the natives called to the admiral and begged him to command that a bell be set aside for them until the next day, because they would bring him four pieces of gold, each as large as a man's hand; the admiral rejoiced at hearing this. Later, a sailor who had come from the shore told the admiral that it was an astonishing thing that the Christians who were on shore were obtaining the pieces of gold in trade for practically nothing: for a metal-tipped lacing, the natives had given pieces of gold that were larger than two *castellanos;*[14] but that then, that was nothing, compared to what it would be a month hence. The king was greatly pleased at seeing the admiral happy, and he understood that the admiral wanted a great deal of gold; and he told him by means of gestures that he knew where there was a lot of it, in great quantity, nearby, and that the admiral should take heart, for he would give him as much gold as the admiral might wish. Concerning this, the admiral says the king gave him an explanation, in particular that there was gold in Cipangu (which they called Cibao),[15] to such an extent that the inhabitants consider it worthless, and that he would bring it here—even though there also is much more on that island Hispaniola (which they call *bohío*) and in that province of Caribata. The king ate aboard the caravel with the admiral, and afterward went ashore with him, where he did the admiral much honor and gave him a meal of two or three

---

[14]A *castellano* was a gold coin equal to 490 silver *maravedís* or 1.31 Venetian ducats; the Venetian ducat weighed 3.5 grams, so the *castellano* weighed approximately 4.6 grams.

[15]Now the interior region of the Dominican Republic.

kinds of *ajes* [sweet potatoes] along with shrimp and game and other foods that they had, and some of their bread that they called cassava [manioc] bread. Then they took him to see some green trees near the buildings, and a good thousand people, all naked, walked along with him. The lord already was wearing the shirt and gloves that the admiral had given him, and he rejoiced more over the gloves than he did over any other of the things the admiral had given him. In his table manners, his decorousness, and his beautiful habit of cleanliness, he showed himself indeed to be of noble lineage. After the king had eaten—for he lingered at the table quite a while—the natives brought certain herbs with which he rubbed his hands a lot (the admiral believed he was doing it to soften them), and they brought him a jug of water for washing his hands. After they had finished eating, the king brought the admiral to the beach, and the admiral sent for a Turkish bow and a handful of arrows. The admiral had one of the men in his company, who knew how to use it, shoot with it, "and to the lord, since they do not know what weapons are, for they neither have them nor use them, it seemed a great thing." He says, however, that, at the beginning, there was talk about the people from Caniba[16] (whom they call Caribs), who come to capture them, and who carry bows and arrows without iron points; for in all those lands there was no memory of iron or steel or any other metal except gold and copper, although the admiral had seen only a very little copper. The admiral told the king by means of gestures that the monarchs of Castile would command that the Caribs be destroyed, and that they would command them to be brought in with their hands tied. The admiral commanded that a Spanish cannon be fired and an Arab cannon; and seeing the effect that their force had produced and what they had penetrated, the king was left amazed, and when his people heard the shots, they all fell to the ground. They brought the admiral a large mask that had big pieces of gold in its ears and in its eyes and other parts, which the king gave him, along with other jewels of gold that the king himself placed on the admiral's head and around his neck; and to the other Christians who were with him he also gave many things. The admiral received much pleasure and consolation from these things that he was seeing; and the anguish and pain that he had received and felt at the loss of the ship were tempered in him, and he recognized that our Lord had had the ship go aground there, so that he might establish a

[16]Caniba's location is unknown; it was the place from which the Caribs (or cannibals) came to attack the Tainos of Hispaniola.

foothold there. "And from this," he says, "have so many things come to my hand that, truly, it was not a disaster but great good luck. For it is certain," he says, "that if I had not gone aground, I would have gone a long distance without anchoring in this place, for it is placed here within a large bay, with two or three reefs of shoals in it. Nor during this voyage should I have left people here; or, even if I had wanted to leave them, I should not have been able to give them such good resources or so many munitions or so many supplies or materials for a fortress. And it is quite true that many of the people who are exploring this place had begged me and had others beg me to agree to give them permission to stay. Now I have decreed that a tower and a fortress be built, all very well made, and a big moat. Not because I believe this may be necessary on account of these people, for I consider it to go without saying that, with the people I bring with me, I would subdue this entire island, which I believe is bigger than Portugal, and with more than twice the population, but they are naked and without weapons and very cowardly, beyond remedy. But there is good reason that this tower be built and that it be as it is to be, being so far from your highnesses: and it is so that the natives may recognize the ingeniousness of your highnesses' people and what they can do, so that out of love and fear they may obey them. Thus, they will have boards with which to build the whole fortress, and supplies of bread and wine for more than a year, and seeds for sowing, and the ship's boat, and a caulker and a carpenter, a cannon-gunner and a cooper; and many men among them who desire to do much for your highnesses' service, and to please me, by learning where the mine is whence the gold is obtained. Thus it is that everything has turned out perfectly, so that this beginning may be made; and above all, the fact that when the ship ran aground, it was so gently that almost nothing was felt, and there was neither wave nor wind." The admiral says all this. He adds, moreover — to show that it was great good luck and the particular will of God that the ship went aground there, so that he should leave people there — that if it had not been for the betrayal of the ship's master and the crew (who were, all or most of them, from the master's native region), in not wanting to cast the anchor astern to get the ship off, as the admiral had commanded them, the ship would have been saved. Thus, it would not have been possible to explore the land, he says, as it was explored in those days that he stayed there, and as would be done later by those he was intending to leave there. For he always went onwards, with the intention of exploring and not stopping anywhere for more than a day, unless it was on account of a

lack of wind, because the ship, he says, was very heavy and not suitable for the job of exploration. The people of Palos, he says, caused
him to bring such a ship, who did not fulfill what they had promised
to the king and queen: to provide ships that were appropriate for
that voyage, and they did not do it. The admiral concludes by saying
that of everything they had on the ship, not a lacing, a plank, or a
nail was lost, for she remained as sound as when she left port—save
that she was cut open and opened up a bit, to get the cargo containers and all the trade goods out—and the natives placed them all on
shore and guarded them well, as has been said. And he says that he
hopes in God that, upon the return voyage he was intending to make
from Castile, he would find a barrelful of gold, which the people he
was to leave behind would have traded for, and that they would
have found the gold mine and the spicery; and that in such quantity
that, within three years, the monarchs might undertake and pre-
pare to go conquer the Holy Sepulcher [in Jerusalem]. "For thus," he
says, "I swore to your highnesses, that all of the profits of this my
enterprise should be expended upon the conquest of Jerusalem; and
your highnesses laughed and said that it pleased you, and that even
without this oath, you had the same desire." These are the admiral's
words. . . .

FRIDAY, DECEMBER 28

In order to put things in order, and to give a sense of urgency to fin-
ishing the fortress's construction and to the people who were going to
stay behind in it, the admiral went ashore. It seemed to him that the
king had seen him while he was coming in the boat; but the king
quickly entered his own house, pretending otherwise, and sent a
brother of his to receive the admiral. The king's brother took him to
one of the buildings that the king had given to the admiral's crew,
which was the biggest and best one in that village. In it, they had prepared a dais made of the coverings of palm trunks, where they had
the admiral sit down. Then the brother sent a squire of his to tell the
king that the admiral was there, as if the king had not known that he
had arrived. For the admiral believed that the king was pretending
this in order to do him much more honor. When the squire told him
about it, the cacique, says the admiral, began to run to the admiral,
and he placed about the admiral's neck a large piece of flattened gold
that he was carrying in his hand. He stayed there with him until
evening, discussing what he was to do. . . .

MONDAY, DECEMBER 31

This day the admiral busied himself with commanding that water and wood be taken on for the departure for Spain, so that swift notice might be given to the monarchs, so that they might send vessels that would discover what remained to be discovered; because already the business seemed "so great and of such importance that it is astonishing," said the admiral. And he says that he had not wanted to depart until he had seen that entire land, which went on towards the east, and might travel along its entire coast, in order to learn thoroughly the passage from Castile to that place, he says, so as to bring over livestock and other things. . . .

WEDNESDAY, JANUARY 2

In the morning he went ashore to take his leave of King Guacanagarí and to part from him in the name of the Lord, and he gave him one of his own shirts. And he demonstrated to the king the force that the cannons had and the result that they produced, for which reason he commanded that one be loaded and shot at the side of the ship that was aground, for the subject of the Caribs, with whom the natives were at war, had come up opportunely. The king saw how far the cannon-shot went and how the stone went through the side of the ship and went very far out to sea. The admiral also caused a skirmish to be held by armed men from the vessels, telling the cacique that he should not be afraid of the Caribs, even if they did come. The admiral did all this, he says, so that the cacique should consider the Christians he was leaving behind as friends, and so as to make him afraid, that he might fear them. The admiral brought the king to eat with him at the building where he had been staying, along with the other persons who were with the king. The admiral earnestly commended him to Diego de Arana and Pedro Gutiérrez and Rodrigo Escobedo, whom he was leaving jointly as his lieutenants over those people whom he was leaving there, so that everything might be well ordered and governed to the service of God and their highnesses. The cacique showed great affection to the admiral, and a great deal of emotion over his departure, especially when he saw him go to embark. A councilor of that king told the admiral that he had commanded a statue of pure gold be made, as big as the admiral himself, and that ten days hence they were to bring it. The admiral embarked with the intention of leaving right away, but the wind did not give him the opportunity. He left behind on that island Hispaniola (which the Indians called *bohío*) thirty-nine men, together with the fortress, and, he says, many friends of King Guacanagarí; and in charge of them, as his lieutenants, Diego de Arana, a native of Córdoba, Pedro Gutiérrez, keeper of the king's dais and servant of the lord steward, and Rodrigo de Escobedo, a native of Segovia, the nephew of Friar Rodrigo Pérez, with all the powers that he himself held from the monarchs. He left them all the merchandise that the monarchs had commanded them to buy as trade goods—which was a lot, so that the men might barter and trade it for gold—along with everything the ship had carried. He also left them biscuit for a year, and wine, and a lot of artillery; and the ship's boat, so that they, as the sailors that most of them were, might go, when they should see that it was appropriate, to discover the gold mine; so that, upon the return that the admiral would make, he should find a lot of gold, and a place where a town could be established—for the one there was not a harbor to his liking, especially since the gold that the natives were bringing there had come, he says, from the east; and the further they might go to the east, the closer they were to Spain. He also left them seeds to sow and his officials, the scribe and the lieutenant, and among them were a ship's carpenter, a caulker, and a good cannon-gunner, who knows siege engines well, and a cooper, a physician, and a tailor. All, he says, were seamen. . . .

Friday, January 4

As the sun was rising, the admiral raised anchor, with a light wind, with the ship's boat at his bow, on a course to the northwest in order to get outside the reef, by means of another channel, wider than the one through which he entered. That channel and others are very good for going in front of the town of La Navidad; and in that entire area, the deepest bottom he found was from three to nine fathoms. . . .

Wednesday, January 9

At midnight the admiral set sail, with the southeast wind, and sailed to the east-northeast. He arrived at a point that he called Punta Roja, which is exactly sixty miles to the east of Monte Cristi, and he anchored under its shelter in the afternoon, which would be three hours before night fell. He did not dare to leave that place at night because there were many reefs, until these were learned about, for they would be useful later, if they have, as they ought to have, channels through them, and these have great depth, and a good anchorage, safe from all winds. These lands, from Monte Cristi to that place where he anchored, are high, flat, very beautiful countryside; and in back are very beautiful hills that go from east to west, and they are all cultivated and green, so that it is a wonder to see their beauty, and they have many streams of water. In all this land there are many turtles, some of which the sailors took at Monte Cristi when they were coming to lay eggs on shore, and they were very large, like a big wooden shield. On the previous day, when the admiral had gone to the Río del Oro, he said that he saw three mermaids that came very high up out of the sea; but they were not so beautiful as they are depicted, for only after a fashion had human form in their faces.[17] He said that he had seen some on other occasions in Guinea, on the coast of Malagueta.[18] . . .

FRIDAY, MARCH 15

Yesterday, after the sun had set, the admiral sailed his course until morning with little wind, and at the sun's rising he found himself off Saltés; and at the midday hour, with a rising tide, he crossed the Saltés bar into the harbor whence he had departed on August 3 of the previous year. And so, he says, now he was ending this written record; except that he was of a mind to go to Barcelona by sea, in which city, they had given him news, the monarchs were, and this in order to make a report to them of his entire voyage, which our Lord had allowed him to make and has wished to bring to light through him. For certainly, beyond the fact that he knew, and firmly and strongly believed, without reservation, that his high majesty creates all good things—and that everything is good except sin—and that nothing can be achieved or thought of, unless it be with his consent, "I recognize this about this voyage," the admiral says, "that he miraculously has revealed it thus, as can be understood by means of this written record, in the many notable miracles that he has shown during the voyage; and in myself, who have been at Your Highnesses' court for so long, despite opposition and against the better judgment of so many important persons in your household, all of whom were against me, saying that this undertaking was a joke—which I hope in our Lord will be the greatest honor of Christendom, which ever thus has appeared in such an unimportant guise." These are the final words of the admiral Sir Christopher Columbus about his first voyage to the Indies and their discovery.

[17]Columbus probably saw three manatees.
[18]Now Liberia.

Second Voyage, 1493–1496

13

Warrant to Christopher Columbus and Juan Rodríguez de Fonseca Commissioning Them to Outfit the Second Voyage

Barcelona, May 24, 1493

Within two months of Columbus's return to Spain, Fernando and Isabel instructed him to organize another transatlantic voyage. They gave the responsibility for equipping and organizing the voyage to Columbus and to Juan Rodríguez de Fonseca, archdeacon of the cathedral of Seville. As a result of their efforts, a total of seventeen ships with approximately 1,200 to 1,300 men on board departed for the Indies in September 1493.

Sir Fernando and Lady Isabel, by the grace of God king and queen of Castile, León, Aragón, Sicily, Granada, Toledo, Valencia, Galicia, the Balearics, Seville, Sardinia, Córdoba, Corsica, Murcia, Jaén, the Algarve, Algeçiras, Gibraltar, the Canary Islands, count and countess of Barcelona, lords of Vizcaya and Molina, dukes of Athens and Neopatria, counts of Roussillon and Cerdagne, marquises of Oristano and Goceano.

To you, Sir Christopher Columbus, our admiral of our islands and mainland that by our order have been and will be discovered in the Ocean Sea in the region of the Indies, and to you, Sir Juan de Fonseca, archdeacon of Seville and member of our council, greetings.

You are informed that we have decided to order a fleet of several ships formed and sent to the Indies, both to secure jurisdiction over these islands and mainland, of which possession has been taken in our name, and to discover others. In order to form this fleet, outfit it with

Helen Nader, ed. and trans., Luciano Formisano, ed., *The Book of Privileges Issued to Christopher Columbus by King Fernando and Queen Isabel 1492–1502,* Repertorium Columbianum 2 (Berkeley: University of California Press, 1996), 79–82.

equipment and stores, and provision it with all things needed and appropriate, we will appoint and delegate persons necessary to be responsible for it and get it started.

Trusting that you will protect our best interests by doing well, faithfully, and diligently what we order you to do, we command that this our warrant be given to you for this purpose. By this warrant we order that you go to the cities of Seville and Cádiz, and any other cities, towns, villages, and seaports of their respective archdiocese and diocese that you consider appropriate, and cause to be leased and bought, and you yourself may buy and lease, any ships, cargo carriers, caravels, and vessels that you think will suffice and are appropriate for this fleet, from any person or persons. If you are not able to obtain them in this way, seize them, even though they are leased to other persons, with as little damage as possible.

Once these cargo carriers, ships, caravels, and vessels have been bought and leased, you can outfit, equip, and supply them with arms and munitions, also provisioning them with weapons, ammunition, supplies, and cannons; soldiers and seamen, sails and rigging and any masters of trades that are necessary whom you see and believe are competent. You may take ships from any places, vessels wherever you find them, paying their owners the reasonable prices they should expect to receive for them. Likewise, you may compel and oblige any masters of any trade that are deemed necessary for going on this fleet to do so. They will be paid the reasonable wages and salary that they ought to have.

It is our wish and command that a description and account of all this be kept so that, when we wish to send for it, it may be entered in our books kept by our chief accountants. Anything relating to this fleet shall be done and approved by Juan de Soria, secretary of Prince Sir Juan, our most dear and very beloved son, who will go as our deputy chief accountant, and by his authority and in no other manner.

It is our wish and command that everything relating to the purchase of arms, munitions, provisions, and other things; the leasing of ships; and other expenses of this fleet, shall be done and approved by our clerk's deputy, whom we now appoint for this fleet, together with Juan de Soria, deputy of our chief accountants. Likewise, so that there shall be no fraud or deception in the wages paid to the personnel who go in this fleet, it is our desire that the muster and appointments of these personnel be made in the presence of our clerk's deputy, and that by his warrant, signed with his name, the admiral and Sir Juan de Fonseca shall authorize the payment of all that has been described.

This deputy of our chief accountants shall sign these vouchers because he is responsible for their records and accounts. Whoever has to make a payment shall not pay anything without a warrant or pay voucher from the admiral and Sir Juan de Fonseca, signed by this deputy chief accountant.

Should it be necessary for you to have preferment and aid in order to do, carry out, and implement all or any part of this, with this our warrant we command any municipal councils, royal judges and governors, municipal judges, sheriffs, councilmen, commissioned and non-commissioned officers, masters of trades, and voting citizens; masters of ships and vessels; and any other persons required by this, to give preferment and aid to you well and fully, and not to obstruct or oppose you in any way, under pain of our displeasure, loss of their offices, and confiscation of all their property for each person who does the contrary. Furthermore, we command the man who shows you this warrant to summon you to appear before us in our court, wherever we may be, within fifteen days of having been cited, under the same penalty. Under this same penalty, we command any public clerk summoned for this purpose to give the man who shows this warrant to you a certificate to that effect inscribed with your rubric, so that we may know how well our command is obeyed.

Given in the city of Barcelona on the twenty-fourth day of the month of May in the year of the birth of our Lord Jesus Christ one thousand four hundred ninety-three. I, the King. I, the Queen. I, Fernán Alvarez de Toledo, secretary of the king and queen our lords, had this written by their order.

14

MICHELE DA CUNEO

From *News of the Islands of the Hesperian Ocean Discovered by Sir Christopher Columbus of Genoa*

October 1495

Born in 1450 in Savona, Italy, Michele da Cuneo was well educated and spoke Genoese, Latin, Castilian, and Tuscan. His father, Corrado da Cuneo, in 1474 sold real estate to Columbus's father, and apparently Columbus and Michele da Cuneo were good friends. Possibly motivated by scientific curiosity, Michele accompanied Columbus on his second voyage; these selections are from a letter written in 1495 after his return to Italy.

On 25 September 1493 we departed from Cádiz with seventeen vessels in excellent order with regard to every thing, that is, fifteen square-rigged and two lateen vessels, and on 2 October we reached Grand Canary. The following night we set sail and on the fifth of the same month we reached Gomera, one of the Canary Islands. If I were to tell you all we did there, what with the parading and bombard shots and fireworks, it would be too long to tell. This was done because of the lady of the place with whom our lord admiral had once been in love.[1] There we supplied ourselves with what we needed. On 10 October we set sail on our direct course, but due to contrary weather we remained three days longer in the vicinity of the Canary Islands. On the morning of 13 October, a Sunday, we left behind the island of Hierro, the last of the Canary Islands and our course was west by south. On 26 October, the eve of Saints Simon and Jude, at about 4 p.m. a sea storm hit us in such a way that you would never have believed it. We thought our days had come to an end. It lasted all night until dawn in such a way that one ship lost sight of the other. Finally, as pleased

---

[1]This is a reference to Beatriz de Bobadilla, although it is probably not true that Columbus had been in love with her.

Geoffrey Symcox and Luciano Formisano, eds., Theodore J. Cachey Jr. and John C. McLucas, trans., *Italian Reports on America 1493–1522: Accounts by Contemporary Observers,* Repertorium Columbianum 12 (Turnhout, Belgium: Brepols, 2002), 50–63.

God, we regrouped and on 3 November, a Sunday, we sighted land, that is, five unknown islands. Our lord admiral named the first Dominica for the day, Sunday, on which it was discovered; the second Mariagalante for love of the ship in which he sailed, which was called *María la Galante.* The two islands were not very large; nevertheless the lord admiral charted them. If I remember well, from the island Hierro to the island Mariagalante it took us twenty-two days, but I believe with a good wind one could cross over easily in sixteen days.

We obtained water and firewood at that island Mariagalante, which is uninhabited though it is filled with trees and level. We sailed from there that same day and reached a big island populated by Cannibals, who, upon sighting us, immediately fled to the woods. We landed on that island and stayed there about six days, and the reason was that eleven of our men joined in a raiding party and went five or six miles into the wilderness, so that when they wished to turn back, they were unable to find their way, even though they were all sailors and observed the sun, which they could not see well because of the thick and dense bush. In this situation, the lord admiral, observing that those men did not return and could not be found, sent 200 men divided into four squads, with trumpets, horns and lanterns; and still with all this, they could not be found, and there was a moment when we feared more for the 200 than for the initial eleven. But the 200 returned (as pleased God) exhausted and very hungry. We believed the eleven had been eaten by those Cannibals, who are accustomed to doing that.

Nevertheless, at the end of five or six days, those eleven, as pleased God, although they had almost lost hope of ever finding us, made a fire above a cape. Sighting the fire we believed it was them, and we sent the boat to them, and by this means they were rescued. If it had not been for an old woman who showed them by signs the way, they were done for, because we intended to continue our voyage the following day. On that island we seized twelve beautiful and very fat females, aged between fifteen and sixteen, with two boys of the same age whose genital members had been cut away clean to the belly. We figured that they had done it to keep them from mixing with their women or perhaps to fatten them up and eat them later. These boys and girls had been captured by the Cannibals; we sent them to Spain as an exhibit for the king. The lord admiral named that island Santa María de Guadalupe.[2]

---

[2] Now Guadeloupe.

On 10 November we set sail from Guadalupe, which is occupied by the Cannibals, and on the fourteenth of that month we reached another beautiful and lush Cannibal island and made our way to a fine harbor. As soon as the Cannibals sighted us they fled toward the woods, just as they had done on the other island; they abandoned their houses, which we proceeded to and took whatever we wished. In those few days we discovered many islands where we did not land, but sometimes stood at anchor, that is, at night, and when we did not stand at anchor we kept the ship hove-to, in order to avoid drifting and running into those islands, which, as they were so many and so close together, the lord admiral called the 11,000 Virgin Islands, and he named the island mentioned before Santa Cruz.

One of those days while standing at anchor we saw a canoe (that is, a boat, for that is what they call it in their language) approaching from around a cape, with such a beating of oars as to look like a well-manned brigantine. There were three or four Cannibal men with two Cannibal women aboard, and two captured Indian slaves (as the Cannibals call their neighbors from the other islands) whose genital members they had also recently cut away clean to the belly so that they were still ailing. Since we were ashore with the captain's boat, as soon as we saw that canoe coming, we promptly jumped into the boat and gave chase to the canoe. As we were getting close to it, the Cannibals shot at us fiercely with their bows, so that had it not been for our shields they would have wounded half our number. You must know that one of the seamen who held a shield in his hand was struck by an arrow which passed through the shield and entered three fingers deep into his chest, so that he died in a few days. We captured that canoe as well as all those men, and one of the Cannibals was wounded by a lance in such a way that we thought he was dead; after leaving him for dead in the sea, we saw him suddenly start swimming. At this we seized him with the grapple and pulled him over the ship's edge where we cut off his head with a hatchet. We later sent the other Cannibals, together with the slaves, to Spain. While I was in the boat I laid my hands on a gorgeous Cannibal woman whom the lord admiral granted me; when I had her in my quarters, naked, as is their custom, I felt a craving to sport with her. When I tried to satisfy my craving, she, wanting none of it, gave me such a treatment with her nails that at that point I wished I had never started. At this, to tell you how it all ended, I got hold of a rope and thrashed her so thoroughly that she raised unheard-of cries that you would never believe. Finally we were of such accord that, in the act, I can tell you, she seemed to have been trained in a school of harlots. The lord admiral gave that cape the name Cabo de la Flecha because of the man who died there from the arrow. . . .

On 27 November we set sail for Monte Santo, where on his other voyage the admiral had left thirty men, and that same night we came to the very place. On 28 November we landed and found all of our men dead and still lying here and there on the ground, without eyes. We thought the islanders had eaten them, for as soon as they have killed anyone, they immediately gouge out his eyes and eat them. They seemed to have been dead between fifteen and twenty days. We met the lord of that place, Guacanagarí, who, with tears falling upon his breast (and likewise all of his men), told us that Caonabó, the lord of the mountains, had come with 3,000 men and had killed them, as well as some of Guacanagarí's own men, and had robbed them in order to vex him. We found nothing of what the lord admiral had left. Hearing this, we believed what they told us. We engaged in those discussions for ten days, and on December 8 we departed from that place because it was unhealthy on account of the marshes there, and we went to another location on the same island, to an excellent harbor, where we landed. There we built 200 houses, small like the huts we use for bird hunting, covered with grass.

When we had built this settlement for us to live in, the inhabitants of the island, from as far as two leagues away, came to see us as if we were their brothers, saying that we were men of God come from heaven, and they stood there a long time admiring and contemplating us, and they brought us some of the things they eat, and we presented them with some of ours; in such a way that we acted like brothers. Here was our voyage's end and destination, although below I will tell about another voyage that I made with the lord admiral when he decided to seek mainland. But now we will speak of other matters, and first, about the search for gold on the island of Hispaniola.

After already having rested many days in our settlement, it seemed to the lord admiral time to put into effect his intention to search for gold, which above all had caused him to undertake such a voyage filled with so many dangers, as you will see more fully in the end. Therefore, the lord admiral sent two captains with about forty men, in good order, and two Indians familiar with the island, to a place called Cibao, where he believed, according to Ptolemy, there was much gold in the rivers. Those men, on the way, crossed a great river, wider and more mighty than that of Seville, and they continually found many hamlets of those Indians who always received them well. In the neighborhood of that Cibao, as there was bad weather and it was necessary to cross another very violent river and we were uncertain of our ability to cross it, we turned around and went back to the nearest settlement, where we conversed with the people. They told us that there positively was gold in great quantities in Cibao, and they presented some gold to our captains in three large nuggets, that is, one worth nine *castellanos,* one fifteen *castellanos,* and another twenty-two, embedded in a piece of rock. They brought this gold to the lord admiral, recounting to him all that we have reported, just as they had heard and seen it. At this point the admiral and the rest of us celebrated grandly, no longer caring at all about any spices, but only about that blessed gold. For this reason the lord admiral wrote to the king that he hoped to give him in a short time as much gold as the mines of Biscay gave him iron. This is what happened then.

In the month of February, after the twelve caravels dispatched by the lord admiral had departed for Spain, 500 of us went together with the lord admiral to Cibao, not too well-supplied with clothing. We were out twenty-nine days on that journey, between coming and going and stopping there, in terrible weather with bad food and worse drink. Nevertheless, thanks to the lust for that gold, all remained strong and hearty. Both coming and going we crossed two very large rivers, as I said above, by swimming, and whoever did not know how to swim had two Indians who carried him across while swimming. The Indians, for love and for a few trifles which we gave them, also carried across our possessions, weapons, and all there was to carry on top of their heads. We finally arrived at Cibao and quickly built a wooden fort named Santo Tomás, which was impregnable to the Indians. It is approximately twenty-seven leagues from our settlement. Many times we fished in those rivers, but no one ever found a single grain of gold. Because of this we were unhappy with the Indians of that place, who all told us that the gold was in the power of the king Caonabó, who lived about two leagues away from our fort. While we were at the fort, many Indians came from as far away as ten leagues to see us, bringing with them some of the gold which they had to show us; they negotiated with us in such a way that we collected about 2,000 *castellanos* worth of gold. In that gold there were some grains of the weight of twenty-four *castellanos* and also gold of another quality, like pure gold. None of us went to find the king Caonabó, because we lacked clothing. It is said that king can summon 50,000 men. Besides the deals made for the aforesaid value of 2,000 *castellanos,* there were other deals secretly made, against our rule and statute, for the value of about 1,000 *castellanos*. As you know, the devil causes one to do ill, then lets it be discovered; also, as long as Spain is Spain, there will be no shortage of traitors. One man betrayed another until they were all discovered, and those found guilty were well flogged, and this one had his ears cut off and that one his nose, such that it was a pity to see.

·   ·   ·

I will now tell you about the voyage I made together with the lord admiral seeking other islands and mainland.[3] You must then know that on 25 April we set sail from our settlement with three caravels; one of these was nearly sixty tons and the other two were very small, and we had with us, including good and bad, ninety-eight men. Going along the coast of Hispaniola, after nearly seventy leagues we discovered a very beautiful island to the north which has a circumference of approximately fifty leagues. The lord admiral gave it the name La Tortuga, and this was because we found there a big turtle. We coasted that island sailing to the west, and after nearly thirty leagues we discovered land which we judged to be mainland. For this reason the lord admiral called a council to discuss which direction to take, and all agreed that it was better to keep to a southerly course, since, if there was anything of value there it would more likely be found to the south than to the north. In the name of God we sailed the coast now to the west, then west by southwest, now southwest by south, following the position of the capes. After sailing nearly sixty leagues we found a very estimable harbor in which there were five very big canoes and all were filled with very big fish of every kind, as described above.

There were Indian men ashore in this harbor sleeping on the sand, who, when they heard the report of our cannons, fled to the mountains. We then sent our interpreter to them to tell them that we were good friends, and very soon they came to us. When we landed we found fifteen or sixteen containers of cooked fish and fifty or sixty of serpents [iguanas], also cooked, which were the size of young goats. We also found between thirty-six and thirty-eight live serpents leashed with cord like monkeys. We talked to the Indians and we asked them why they were cooking so much fish. They answered us that the fish could be preserved that way; otherwise it would be impossible since they intended to send the fish to their settlements which were five, six and ten leagues distant. We gave them some of our things, and we

---

[3]These passages describe Columbus's exploration of Cuba and Jamaica in 1494.

asked them if there was gold in those parts. They answered no, but that it was certainly true that there was much of it on an island called Jamaica, which was south by south east from there. We asked them if they ever went to that island. They said no, because whoever went there would never return, since he would be drowned either coming or going. We asked them nevertheless if it was far. They answered, "five suns," that is, five days.

We sailed along the coast to go to the island of Jamaica where they had told us we would find the blessed gold; in very bad weather, with the sails down, we crossed to that island, which we estimated to be about 150 miles away. We went to an excellent harbor, which was well populated. As soon as we were anchored there, nearly sixty canoes immediately surrounded us. Seeing this, we discharged ten or twenty blank cannon shots, and, hearing the noise, they all fled toward shore. When we tried to land they threw stones at us, so that the boats had to return to the ships. We then equipped the boats with shields, cross-bows, and cannons and headed in the direction of land. They greeted us as before, and at that point we immediately killed sixteen or eighteen of them with the crossbows and five or six with the cannons. This took place about shortly after vespers,[4] and we returned late to the caravels. We went back the next day to fight, but those men, holding their arms, as it were, in a cross, begged mercy of us and brought to us all of their possessions, including bread of the type described in great quantities, fish, roots, and gourds filled with water. They also brought some of their own weapons. We went ashore then and presented to them some of our things; among these were bells that they received more willingly than anything else and immediately placed in their ears and noses. The ears and noses, that is, the septum, of both men and women, are all pierced for that purpose. We asked them about gold, and they answered that they did not know about it, nor had they ever seen it.

We remained in that harbor four full days for repairs. In the interim 60,000 persons came down from the mountains just to see us, all of them naked, speaking one language, and they said that we were men from the other world. We set sail and went along the coast of that island for approximately seventy leagues, always encountering the same trees and things as on the other islands.

---

[4]Time was given in canonical hours, which corresponded to religious services throughout the day; vespers is the canonical hour that corresponds to sunset or early evening.

We turned back toward land, and after sailing approximately 200 leagues along the coast, we discovered an archipelago in a white sea, where there are numerous islands and the water is quite shallow, at most between twelve and twenty-five spans[5] far from shore, while near land the depth is no more than twelve or thirteen to fifteen spans. The sea is white because the bottom is made of chalk. Those islands are in part inhabited, in part uninhabited. The people of these islands are in our judgment somewhat darker than on the other islands. Their principal food is fish, and they drink seawater, lacking fresh water because the islands are very low and level, without mountains, and are also far from the mainland, which causes the waters to be brackish. The same is true of another archipelago that I will tell you about shortly.

Having navigated in this white sea eighteen or twenty days without finding anything of value, we headed out to sea, to get out from the shallow waters, and found the sea to be of normal depth. After sailing nearly six days, always within sight of those islands, we found the coast of the mainland, which we followed and found a very beautiful and excellent harbor. Recently a fire had been made ashore, and we judged that fishermen had been there. We took on provisions, which we greatly needed because for twelve days we had been rationed to a cup of water and some of the bread made of turnips [cassava] mentioned earlier. . . .

Thus, having taken on our provisions, we returned to our course and sailed along the coast west by southwest, for the lord admiral believed this to be mainland. After pointing the prow to the north into a gulf, we decided it was an island. We returned to the west by southwest course, and after sailing approximately sixty leagues we sighted land; thus seen, we thought it was mainland. Then sailing northwest to find Cathay, following the opinion of the lord admiral, we found it to be a gulf. Seeing this, we turned and returned to our original course, sailing always along the coast, sometimes to starboard, sometimes to port, and discovered another white archipelago like the first. We continued along the coast, which was always inhabited, and did not find anything new, but only the usual, and the same throughout the previously mentioned archipelago; and just as in the other, we found abundant fish in the sea of the kinds mentioned above, and very large conches, as big as the head of an ox, with a mollusk as large as a man's arm. They can be seen on the bottom like rocks. There were also endless numbers of crayfish. We took boatloads of these conches

---

[5]A span was a linear measurement equivalent to about nine inches.

and cooked them in seawater; they made excellent eating. We also found in that white sea many large oysters between one and four spans long and a span and a half wide. Seeing them, we truly thought we had become rich men. We collected perhaps five or six boatloads and opened all of them without finding a single pearl; nevertheless they were very good to eat.

We remained in that archipelago thirty-seven days, sailing along the coast. We would have followed our course further if it had not been for the lack of depth. Therefore, everything considered, it seemed to us better to turn around and return across this same archipelago, and God knows how much trouble we had getting out of it. We headed out to sea leaving the first archipelago behind to the northwest and entered the high seas, sailing approximately fifteen days without ever discovering land of any kind. At this we all began to grumble, saying that we were going to be drowned and that we did not have enough food. When the lord admiral heard this, he ordered that we turn in the direction of land, to the aforesaid island of Jamaica, named by the lord admiral San Diego, where we remained approximately seventeen days and took on provisions.

From there we headed in the direction of Hispaniola, which we judged to be approximately forty leagues away from this island. We nearly circled Jamaica completely and did not find anything any better than what we found in the other islands. . . . On the last day of September, in God's name, we safely reached Isabela, our settlement, where we found all of our men greatly afraid for us, believing us all to be dead. Besides this, there were many men ill and undernourished. Seeing this, the lord admiral sent approximately 500 men throughout the island for provisions. But within a few days, as pleased God, four caravels arrived from Spain, loaded with provisions, which greatly comforted the company. Sailing up and down, we nearly circled Hispaniola and that other island Jamaica; as a result we estimated Hispaniola to have a circumference of 600 leagues and Jamaica 700, and this is for your information. During that time, after we had departed from Hispaniola, our unplanned course, seeking new islands and mainland, was always to the west, or west by south.

When our caravels were ready to depart for Spain, aboard which I intended to return home, we gathered at our settlement 1,600 Indians, male and female; we loaded 550 of the best—both men and women—aboard those caravels on 17 February 1495. Regarding the rest, it was declared that whoever wanted some of them could take them as he wished, and so it was. When everyone was supplied, approximately

400 still remained who were permitted to go wherever they liked. Among those were many females with nursing infants, who, so as to better escape from us, fearing that we would return to take them, abandoned their children to their fate, leaving them on the ground and fleeing like desperate persons. They fled so far that they distanced themselves seven or eight days from Isabela, our settlement, beyond mountains and great rivers, so that it will be nearly impossible to take them in the future. Among the captives was one of their kings with two principal men; it was decided that they should be executed with arrows the following day. For this purpose they were shackled, but that night they were so adept at gnawing at one another's heels with their teeth that they escaped from the shackles and fled. The news of this capture and the loading of people aboard the caravels came to the notice of King Guacanagarí, neighbor to our settlement, who sent an ambassador to King Caonabó, his superior, to inform him of the matter. King Caonabó commanded him to go personally to the lord admiral to hear why he had done this. But King Guacanagarí, fearing for his own safety, did not go to him, but sent two of his own most wise and eloquent men to the lord admiral to inform him of the situation. But the lord admiral sent word that Guacanagarí himself should come so that he could better explain everything to the king.

In the meantime I departed for Spain aboard those caravels; we sailed in heavy and contrary weather and it was necessary to turn back three times, so that we passed a month among those islands. For this reason, seeing that we had few provisions, we set our course to the north, and proceeded approximately 600 miles; as pleased God we had such favorable winds that we passed from the island of Boriquén[6] all the way to the island of Madeira in twenty-three days. But by the time we had reached Spanish waters, approximately 200 of the Indians had died—I believe it was because they were unaccustomed to the air which is colder than theirs—and we cast them into the sea. The first land we sighted was Cape Spartel and very soon after we reached Cádiz, where we unloaded all of the slaves, half of whom were sick. For your information, they are not men made for work, and they fear greatly the cold and do not live long.

About the matter of your friend Sir Bartolomé, brother of the lord admiral, about whom you have insistently asked me, I say that recently he was named adelantado of those countries by the lord

---

[6]Puerto Rico.

admiral.[7] The adelantado is planning to depart with two caravels and a small galley, built in Hispaniola, to go exploring to the north during the entire month of April. If he does not find more than what we found in those parts, according to the above, I fear it will be necessary to abandon them, for when I was in Seville, his majesty the king declared that whoever wanted to go to the islands, could go there, if they would give him one-fifth of what was obtained. This is a sign that the king does not think much of them. We are fairly certain that Lord Bartolomé sailing 500 leagues to the northern regions will find land, but he will also find bigger storms and worse weather than we encountered. The lord admiral says that he will find Cathay. He disputed this point at length with an abbot of Lucena, a very knowledgeable and very rich man who came alone to those regions for his pleasure, to see new things. This man is a good astronomer and cosmographer. Discussing that coast which we mentioned above, the one we navigated for 550 leagues, he, that is, the abbot, denied that because of its size it was mainland and said that it was a very big island. The majority of us, considering the course of our voyage, agreed with this opinion. For this reason the lord admiral did not want to let him return to Spain with us, since if he were asked his opinion by his majesty the king, he might with his answer cause the king to abandon the enterprise. The admiral will keep him there until the return of the adelantado, who will report what he has found.

But one thing I want you to know is that, in my humble opinion, since Genoa was Genoa there has never been a man so courageous and astute in the act of navigation as the lord admiral, for, when sailing, by simply observing a cloud or a star at night, he judged what was to come, if there was to be bad weather. He himself commanded and stood at the helm. When the storm had passed, he raised the sails while the others slept. Likewise, before we reached the "big" island [Guadeloupe] he said these words to us: "Gentlemen, I want to lead you to a place from which one of the three kings who came to venerate Christ departed, and that place is called Saba." When we had reached that place and asked the name they told us it was called Sobo. At that point the admiral said that it was the same word but they did

---

[7]Bartolomé Colón (1461–1514 or 1515), the third son of Columbus's father, Domenico Colombo, was his brother's devoted supporter. He arrived in Hispaniola on June 24, 1494; appointed by Columbus to the office of adelantado (governor), he governed Hispaniola in Columbus's absence.

not pronounce it very well. In that place we captured two men, one of whom was cacique, that is, king, and he gave us many presents. When he wanted to return to land, the lord admiral did not permit it, saying that he wanted to use him in exploring and that thereafter he would give him leave. At that point the king, indicating heaven with his finger, answered that it was God in heaven who rendered justice to all men and that he appealed for justice before him in time. In our eyes he was a very discerning man.

Nothing else is required for this letter, except that I am at your lordship's service. Completed at Savona on the 28th day of this month. Your Michele da Cuneo.

15

GIAMBATTISTA STROZZI

Letter from Cádiz

March 19, 1494

This letter by Giambattista Strozzi and the following by Giovanni de' Bardi were written by Italians from Cádiz and Seville, respectively. They were presumably merchants who would have been in a privileged position to learn the news brought back by the first ships to return from the second voyage to the Indies, in March 1494. Strozzi's report on the islands' position does not make sense and probably represents deliberate misinformation to keep the location of the newly found islands secret.

On the seventh of this month there arrived here in safety twelve caravels which came from the new islands found by Columbus, admiral of the Ocean, for the king of Castile, having come in twenty-five days from the said islands of the Antilles by steering northeast to north; they arrived directly here at Cádiz at the twenty-third hour without ever finding any other land; these islands extend more than forty-

Geoffrey Symcox and Giovanna Rabitti, eds., Peter D. Diehl, trans., *Italian Reports on America 1493–1522: Letters, Dispatches, and Papal Bulls,* Repertorium Columbianum 10 (Turnhout, Belgium: Brepols, 2001), 43.

three degrees, from twenty-six degrees north to thirty-one degrees below the equator, according to report. They brought with them gold worth about 30,000 ducats, according to what they say; much cinnamon, but white like Arabian ginger; pepper in pods like the broad bean, very strong but not substantial like that from the Levant; logs which they say are sandalwood, but white; parrots like falcons and red like pheasants. They found trees which make fine wool, trees which make wax, and trees which make raw cotton; and many brown men with wide faces like Tartars, with hair extending to the middle of their shoulders, large and very quick and fierce, and they eat human flesh and children, and castrated men whom they keep and fatten like capons, and then they eat them; the aforesaid are called Cannibals. In the said islands there are no four-footed animals, nor grain, nor wine, and they live from the ears of grass and fruits and human flesh; and thus they have found islands like those of the Amazons who have men at their command. This next voyage will make known everything. Giambattista Strozzi, in Cádiz.

16

GIOVANNI DE' BARDI

Letter from Seville

April 19, 1494

Like Strozzi, Giovanni de' Bardi was a member of a prominent family of Florentine merchants. His letter offers more detailed information than Strozzi's, and it shows how news from the Americas quickly spread across Europe through personal correspondence. Note the particular attention Bardi gives to reports of encounters with cannibals.

The caravels departed from Cádiz on the twenty-fourth of September, and on the thirteenth of October they sighted the island of Hierro,

Geoffrey Symcox and Giovanna Rabitti, eds., Peter D. Diehl, trans., *Italian Reports on America 1493–1522: Letters, Dispatches, and Papal Bulls,* Repertorium Columbianum 10 (Turnhout, Belgium: Brepols, 2001), 43–45.

and on the third of November with the name of God they saw land and islands without number, and to recount the entire voyage would be a long tale to tell, but I promise you that I will send you a copy of the letter written by the admiral and another which goes to our lord the prince, from which you will learn in detail what they found day by day; in this one I will make a summary of the most important matters.

Consider it certain that they have found six rivers which all bear a great quantity of gold, which rivers are in an island which is called Hispaniola; that forty men went inland for twenty leagues and with great fear they gathered twenty marks[1] worth of gold of that which certainly appears to originate and come from the rivers; they had the word of the said Indians that two days further was the true mine, showing with signs that there was such a great quantity that it seems to be lying to say it; and we saw a very good sign to believe that this may be the truth, because we find that all those who have come here, who were at the said rivers, have brought stolen gold and so much that it has been sold for 150 *castellanos;* and consider this certain, because we have seen it with our own eyes. Also, they bring an infinite variety of samples of spices and aromatic woods and sandalwoods, which would be tedious to enumerate, and when there is time, a copy of everything will be sent to you. Also, the said caravels carry twenty-six Indians of diverse islands and languages; it is true that they are almost the same height, among whom there are three Cannibals of those who live on and eat human flesh, and they are of about the same type as the Indians, save that they are much stronger and fiercer than the others. And they say that these live on an island which is called Camulán;[2] they sail in certain boats made in one piece from a tree, and they row with certain paddles, and they have seen boats which hold forty or fifty of them; they say that when they saw our kind of ships, all of them fled to the mountain. And going along the coast they saw a boat with nine Cannibals, five men and four women, and at once the captain sent a boat to meet them; and as soon as they saw the boat coming, they set their course for land; in the end they caught up to them, and they defended themselves from the Christians and wounded two of our men. At the end they rammed them, and as soon as they collided, the men and women threw themselves into the sea as if they were fishes, and going to catch them, they defended them-

---

[1]The mark *(marco)* was a weight approximately equal to 230 grams.
[2]Possibly a reference to Boriquén, now Puerto Rico.

selves. Our men saw two noteworthy things about them: one is that one of the men, who had a wound in his body from which his entrails came out and two other wounds in the shoulders, still swam and held in his guts with his hands; at the end they slew him with lance-thrusts. The other was that a woman while swimming shot an arrow with a bow and skewered a Biscayan from front to back; and they say that another pierced a shield. And so they caught four of them, and the others escaped by swimming. And later the Spaniards were on land at their houses, and they found that they kept certain slaves, whom they had castrated so that they could fatten them up to eat them; and he came back with three of them, that is two whose virile members had been cut off, and one whose testicles had been cut off, so that you would judge them to be women. And they found many heads and bones in their houses; they say that they have eaten them all; and here in our house we find twelve Indians, whom they have to send to the king, and who are three eunuchs, three Cannibals, and six Indians. Item, they bring, as we can say from seeing them, sixty parrots of various colors, among which there are eight that are as large as falcons, and they are the most beautiful kind of birds that fly through the air. Item, they bring certain animals like rabbits [guinea pigs], half black and half white, except that they do not have any trace of a tail and they have large ears; they say that they did not see any land animals, except the aforesaid, and three others like a dog, but they did not bring them. They relate that those who went to discover the mine got lost in a forest where the trees were so high that one hardly saw the sky; and they say that if it were not for some of them who climbed to the top of them so that they could discern the greater part of the sky, that they would never have come out. They say that they have discovered up to now 150 islands, and that there are yet many more; and they relate that there are many other things of which there is not enough time to tell, promising that when they have more time, they will send an account of everything.

Third Voyage, 1498–1500

17

Instructions to Columbus for Colonization of the Indies
Burgos, April 23, 1497

In April through July of 1497 Fernando and Isabel issued a series of writs containing orders for Columbus's third voyage to the Indies; their major objective was the colonization of Hispaniola. The following document specifies that Columbus was to take 330 settlers, including farmers, gold miners, and laborers, and specifies their provision and remuneration. It is the first royal writ to mention converting the native Americans to Christianity, and it states that the Taino inhabitants should pay an annual per capita tax.

Sir Christopher Columbus, our admiral, viceroy and governor of the Ocean Sea.

In our opinion, the things that must be done and implemented, with the help of God our lord, above and beyond that which, by another of our writs, you and the bishop of Badajoz[1] must provide for the settlement of the Indies and continent discovered and placed under our sovereignty, of those islands and mainland still to be discovered in the region of the Indies in the Ocean Sea, and of the people who, by our command, are already there and will go to live there in the future, are the following:

First. When, God willing, you are in the Indies you shall endeavor with all diligence to encourage and lead the natives of the Indies to

---

[1]Juan Rodríguez de Fonseca (1451–1523), the bishop of Badajoz, was an adviser to the Spanish court. On May 20, 1493, Fernando and Isabel appointed him to create a fleet in Seville for Columbus's second voyage, and thereafter he took the lead in organizing the voyages to the Indies.

Helen Nader, ed. and trans., Luciano Formisano, ed., *The Book of Privileges Issued to Christopher Columbus by King Fernando and Queen Isabel 1492–1502,* Repertorium Columbianum 2 (Berkeley: University of California Press, 1996), 105–8.

serve us and remain benignly under our sovereignty and subjection in peace and order, and especially to convert them to our holy Catholic faith. They and those who are going to live in the Indies shall be administered the holy sacraments by the monks and priests who are already there and those going now, so that God our lord may be served and their consciences may be satisfied.

Item. From now until we order further, 330 persons may go with you, whom you shall choose with such qualifications and professions as stipulated in the instructions. If it seems to you that some of the instructions should be adjusted, however, by adding to some occupations and professions while reducing others, you or your proxy can do so, as you think will contribute to our service as well as the welfare and advantageous governance of the Indies.

Item. When, God willing, you are in the Indies, you shall establish another settlement or fortress on the island of Hispaniola, on the other side of the island from the one already in existence, near the gold mine in the place and form that seems best to you.

Item. Near this new settlement or the one that is already established or in some other location that seems well situated to you, establish and introduce plowing and animal husbandry, so that the persons who are or will be residing on the island can sustain themselves better and more economically. In order best to accomplish this, give to the farmers now going to the Indies up to fifty *cahices*[2] of the wheat and barley being sent there, on loan for sowing, and up to twenty yokes of oxen, mares, or other plow stock. Farmers who receive the grain shall plow, sow, and obligate themselves to return an equivalent amount of grain to you at harvest time in addition to paying the tithe on what is harvested. The farmers may sell the remaining grain to the Christians for as much as they can, provided that the prices do not cause undue hardship for those purchasing it. If the latter should occur, you, our admiral, or your representative must set and enforce a maximum price.

Item. The 330 persons going to the Indies must be paid their wages at the rate that has been paid up to now. Instead of the maintenance that they are usually given, they must be provided with some of the grain that we are ordering sent there: to each person one *fanega*[3] of wheat every month and twelve *maravedís* per day to buy other necessary food. This is to be issued to them by you, our admiral, or your

[2]A *cahiz* is a grain measure, equivalent to 4.78 metric tons.
[3]A *fanega* is a unit of volume that varies between 22.5 and 55.5 liters.

proxy, and the agents of our chief accountants in the Indies. Our treasurer in the Indies shall pay them according to your roster, vouchers, and writs in the stipulated manner.

Item. If you the admiral believe that it would be advantageous to our service if the total number of persons were increased from 330, you may do so up to a total of 500 persons, on the condition that the wages and food of these extra persons are paid from any merchandise and valuables acquired in the Indies, without our ordering provisions for them from elsewhere.

Item. The persons who remain in the Indies shall be paid the wages owed them according to the roster, in the manner stipulated. Those who are not on the payroll are to be compensated for their service as appears best to you, and those who have worked for others likewise.

Item. The posts, salaries, and wages of commanders and other principal persons and officials who live and serve there ought to be remunerated according to what seems proper to you, our admiral, taking into consideration the qualifications of each person and what work each has done and will do. In addition to this, when, God willing, the means to bestow favors in the Indies exists, we shall issue further instructions on how to do so. These shall be awarded by our officials, who will be notified to issue and pay them in the prescribed manner. . . .

Item. Concerning the settlement of estates for those who die in the Indies, it seems to us the procedure should be observed that you described in a section of your report to us, which is as follows: "Many foreigners and citizens have died in the Indies, and I ordered, by virtue of the powers that I have from Your Highnesses, that they should draw up wills and that these should be executed. I gave responsibility to Escobar, citizen of Seville, and Juan de León, citizen of La Isabela, faithfully to discharge all this by paying what the deceased owed, if their executors had not paid it, as well as recovering all their property and wages. All this must be recorded by magistrates and public clerks. Everything accumulated should be placed in a chest with three locks; the executors will have one key, a monk another, and I the third. The money of the deceased shall be placed in this chest and remain there for up to three years, so that the heirs will have time to come for it or send to claim it. If they do not claim it in this time, it should be distributed in good works for their souls."

Likewise, it seems to us that the gold obtained in the Indies should be minted and made into coins of Granada *excelentes*[4] as we have or-

---

[4] An *excelente* was a coin worth two *castellanos,* or 2.62 Venetian ducats, at the time of Fernando and Isabel.

dered in these our kingdoms, in order to avoid the making of counterfeits from this gold in the Indies. In order to coin the money, we order that you take the persons, dies, and tools necessary, for which purpose we give you complete power, with the condition that the money coined in the Indies conforms to the ordinances that we now order to be made about the coining of money. The craftsmen who do the coining must observe these ordinances, under the stipulated penalties.

Item. It seems to us that the Indians who have agreed to pay the ordered tax should wear a token of brass or lead that they can hang from the neck. The design or mark on this token should be changed each time one pays, so that it will be known if someone has not paid. Every time persons are found on the island without this token hanging from the neck, have them arrested and given some light penalty. Because it will be necessary to appoint a diligent and trustworthy person to collect and receive the tribute, it is our wish and command that [*left blank*] should have this office. From the tribute and merchandise that he receives, collects, and causes to be paid, he shall take and keep for himself five weights, measures, or pounds per hundred, which is one-twentieth of what he is to receive and cause to be collected and received. I, the King. I, the Queen. By order of the king and queen. Fernán Alvarez de Toledo.

18

BARTOLOMÉ DE LAS CASAS

On Columbus's Third Voyage

ca. 1527–1563

The source for these selections is chapters 131–33 and 140 of Las Casas's History, *hence the mixture of paraphrasing and direct quotation, as in Columbus's Log. The passages describe Columbus's voyage from the Canary Islands on a more southerly route than before, to Trinidad and the north coast of what is today Venezuela. Columbus was thus the first European to reach South America. He realized that he had found a con-*

Geoffrey Symcox and Jesús Carrillo, eds., Michael Hammer and Blair Sullivan, trans., *Las Casas on Columbus: The Third Voyage*, Repertorium Columbianum 11 (Turnhout, Belgium: Brepols, 2001), 21–146.

tinental landmass and speculated that it might be the location of the Earthly Paradise described in the Bible.

On Wednesday the fourth of July [1498] he gave the order to raise the sails and set out from the island of Santiago [in the Canary Islands] (where he says that after arriving he never saw the sun or the stars, but just skies covered with such a thick fog that it seemed that they could cut it with a knife, and a most intense heat that distressed them). He ordered them—in the name, he says, of the holy and individual Trinity—to take the southwest route, which leads south from those islands; by traveling in that direction they would be on the same latitude as the lands of the Sierra Leone and cape Santa Ana in Guinea, which is below the equator, the parallel of the world below which, he says, more valuable gold is found. And after that he would sail toward the west, if the Lord were willing, and from there to Hispaniola. Along that route he would test King João's theory, mentioned above;[1] and he considered verifying something that the Indians of Hispaniola had said: that black people had come there from the south and the southeast and that their spear tips were made of a metal that they called *guanín*. He had once sent the king and queen an assay that had been done of this metal, where it was found that of thirty-two parts, eighteen were of gold, six of silver, and eight of copper. . . .

Now that they were traveling in good weather, on Sunday the twenty-second of July in the afternoon they saw innumerable birds fly by from the west-southwest toward the northeast. He says that they were an important sign of land. They saw the same thing on the following Monday and successive days, on one of which a pelican came to the admiral's ship. And many others appeared on another day along with other birds that are called frigates. On the seventeenth day of good weather that they had, the admiral hoped to see land because of the birds they had seen. And since he did not see it on Monday or the next day, Tuesday the thirty-first of July, and because he was now out of water, he decided to change his route—which was to the west—and to come alongside on the right and land on Dominica (or one of the Cannibal Islands which today are called the Caribes). And so he gave the order to steer north, one quarter from the northeast, and followed that route until midday. "But as his high majesty," he says, "has always been compassionate with me, by happenstance and by chance,

---

[1]That is, the theory that gold is formed most readily south of the equator.

a sailor from Huelva, a servant of mine named Alonso Pérez, climbed up the mainmast and saw land to the west, fifteen leagues away. What appeared were three knolls or mountains." These are his words.

He named this land the island of Trinidad, because he had determined to give the first land he discovered that name. "And our Lord pleased," he says, "through his great majesty, that the first sight of it was three knolls joined together. I mean three mountains all at one time and in a single view. His immense power through his mercy guides me," he says, "in such a way that he receives much service and Your Highnesses much pleasure, for it is certain that finding this land in this place was a great miracle, as was the discovery on the first voyage." These are his words. . . .

Therefore, having sighted land to the great relief of everyone, he left the route he had wished to follow to search for some Cannibal island in order to take on water, which he needed very much, and turned toward the land that they had seen, toward a cape that appeared to be toward the west, which he named Cabo de la Galera because of a large rock which, from far away, looked like a galley under sail. They arrived there at the hour of compline.[2] They saw a good harbor, however it was not deep, and the admiral regretted that he could not enter it. He continued on toward the point that he had seen, which was seven leagues toward the south, and did not find a harbor. Along the entire coast he found that the forests reached to the sea—the most beautiful thing that eyes had ever seen. He says that this island must be large. Far off a canoe appeared, filled with people who must have been fishing. They fled to shore to some houses that appeared there. The land was well cultivated, high, and beautiful.

On Wednesday the first of August he ran down the coast five leagues toward the west and arrived at a point where he anchored all three of the ships, and they took on water from springs and brooks. They found signs of people, fishing implements, and signs of goats, but these were actually deer, for they are plentiful in those lands. He says that they found aloeswood and palm groves and vast and very beautiful lands, "for which may infinite thanks be given to the holy Trinity." These are his words.

He saw many cultivated areas along the coast and many villages. He saw from there, toward the south or *austro,* another island, the length of which extended more than twenty leagues. This is the mainland, and therefore he discovered the mainland on Wednesday the

[2]Compline is the canonical hour that closes the liturgical day, probably around 9 p.m.

first of August 1498.[3] He could as well have said 500 leagues, because this is the mainland, which, since he saw only a small part, looked like an island to him. He named it Isla Sancta. He says here that he did not want to take any Indians because he did not want to raise an alarm. From Cabo de la Galera to the point where he took on water, which I believe he named Punta de la Playa,[4] he says that, having traveled a great distance and run east-west, there was no harbor in all that way, but it was a very well-populated and well-worked land with lots of water and thick forests—the most beautiful thing in the world—and the trees brushed against the sea. Here it must be noted that when the trees brush against the sea it is a sign that that stretch of sea is not rough. Because when it is rough there are no trees there at all, but rather sand. He says the surging current, which comes from above, and the mounting current, which travels upward from below, appear to be very great. He says the island to the south is very large, because he was in fact discovering the mainland, even though he thought it was an island. He says he was looking for a harbor along the island of Trinidad, on Thursday the second of August, and got as far as the cape of the island of Trinidad, a point which he named Point Arenal,[5] which is to the west. He had now entered the gulf which he called la Ballena,[6] where he was in great danger of losing all his ships. And he still did not know that he was close to the mainland, as will be seen.

This gulf is a marvelous thing and dangerous because of the great river that flows into it, which is called Yuyaparí,[7] with the last syllable long. This river travels more than 300, and I believe 400 leagues, and the 300 have been ascended by ship, by brigantine, and by large canoe. And as it always carries a great amount of water (especially during this season of July and August when the admiral passed through there, which is the wet season, as in Castile during October and November) and thus naturally tends to spill out into the sea, the sea with its similarly great force also tends to break on the shore. And since that gulf is surrounded by mainland on one side and on the

[3]The Italian navigator Amerigo Vespucci (1454–1512) falsely claimed to have explored the South American continent in 1497. The claim was accepted, however, and led the German cartographer Martin Waldseemüller to name the new continent in his honor when he published his map of the world in 1507. Vespucci actually sailed to South America in 1499.

[4]Point Erin.

[5]Point Icacos.

[6]The Gulf of Paria.

[7]The northern branch of the Orinoco river delta.

other by the island of Trinidad and is, as a result, very narrow for the violent force of the opposing waters, they meet in a terrible confrontation and a very dangerous battle. . . .

This Thursday the second of August a large canoe came from the east, carrying twenty-five men. And once they arrived at the distance of a cannon shot, they stopped rowing and shouted out many words. The admiral believed, and I also believe, that they were asking who they were, just as the other people of the Indies usually do. The Spaniards responded, not with words but by showing them some brass pots and other shiny things so that they would come up to the ship, cajoling them with movements and gestures. They came closer and then became frightened of the ship. And, since they did not wish to come closer, the admiral commanded that a drummer go up on the poop deck and that the young men of the ship dance, believing that would please them. But they did not see it that way. Rather, when they saw the drumming and dancing, they took it as a sign of war. And, as if they had been challenged, they dropped their oars and took hold of their bows and arrows, each one embracing his shield and beginning to shoot a sizeable cloud of arrows. Seeing this, the admiral gave the command to stop the fiesta of drumming and dancing and to take out several concealed crossbows and to shoot at the men with two of these, but only to surprise them. The latter, having shot their arrows, went up to one of the caravels and, suddenly, without fear, placed themselves below the stern. And the pilot of the caravel, also without any fear, dangled himself from the stern and dropped down to the canoe with them and gave them some things that he had with him. And among these he gave a robe and a bonnet to one of them who appeared to be the head man. They took him in the canoe, and, as thanks for what he had given them, indicated to him by means of signs that he should come ashore and that there they would bring to him some of what they had. The pilot said that he would, and then they headed for the shore. The pilot got into the ship's boat and went to the admiral's ship to ask his permission. But, because the men in the canoe saw that the pilot was not heading straight toward them, they did not wait for him any longer and left; neither the admiral nor the others ever saw them again.

Because they had been so upset and angered by the drum and the dancing, it seems that, among themselves, they must have taken this as a sign of war. A servant of the admiral named Bernaldo de Ibarra, who came on this voyage with him, told me and gave it to me in writing and today I have it in his writing in my possession that a lord and cacique of the island of Trinidad came to the admiral's ship wearing a diadem of gold on his head, and went to the admiral, who had a crimson cap, and reverenced him and touched his diadem and with the other hand took the cap from the admiral, placing the diadem on the admiral's head and placing on his own head the crimson cap, being very rich and content. . . .

From Point Arenal, which is at the end of the island of Trinidad, he saw a cape or point on the mainland toward the north, a quarter from the northeast at a distance of fifteen leagues, and this was the one which is called Paria. The admiral called it Isla de Gracia, since he believed that it was a different island. He says that this island extends to the west and is a very high land. And he spoke the truth because large and very high mountain ranges run throughout that mainland. On Saturday the fourth of August he decided to go to see Isla de Gracia, and raised anchor and set sail from Point Arenal, where he had been anchored. Since the strait through which he had entered the Golfo de la Ballena was no more than two leagues wide, with Trinidad on one side and the mainland on the other, the fresh water ran out very quickly. A very great current like a vigorous flood came from the south—from the great strength of the Yuyaparí river, which is to the south, although he still had not seen it—toward Point Arenal on the island of Trinidad, with such great thunder and noise that it amazed everyone, and they thought they would not escape from it. The water of the sea resisted it, coming against it in such a way that the sea lifted itself, making a great and very high swell of water which lifted the ship, placing it atop the swell, something which he had never before heard or seen. And it dislodged the anchors of the other ship, which still must not have been weighed, and cast it toward the sea, and it sailed on until it came clear of that swell. The admiral says here that he beseeched God not to cause them any harm. And when he wrote of this to the king and queen he said: "Even today I have fear in my body, for it could have capsized the ship when it came under her." Because of this great danger he named this mouth Serpent's Mouth. Once he had reached the mainland that he had seen in that region and believed to be an island, he saw near the cape two islets in the middle of another opening which form that cape of the mainland, which he named Cabo Boto because it was thick and blunt, and another cape on Trinidad island which he named Cabo de Lapa. He called one of the little islands Caracol and the other Delfín.

This strait, which extends from Cabo de Lapa on Paria to Cabo Boto on Trinidad, is no more than five leagues wide and those two islets lie in the middle. The narrowness of this strait and the impetus of the great Yuyaparí river, combined with the stormy waves of the sea, make entering and leaving very dangerous. And because the admiral tried it, with travail and danger to himself, he called that strait or entrance the Dragon's Mouth, as it is commonly known today. He went along the coast of Paria—which he thought was an island called Isla de Gracia—toward the west to look for a harbor.

The admiral says that it is twenty-six long leagues from Point Arenal, which is a cape of Trinidad, as is said, and is at the southern end, to the other cape, Boto, which is on the same island of Trinidad and faces the sea. This part appears to be the width of the island, and the two capes run from north to south.

There were strong currents, one against another, and many showers poured down on them, since it was the rainy season, as we said above. The admiral says that the Isla de Gracia (which is, as has been said, the mainland) is very high and filled with trees which grow all the way to the sea, since the gulf is surrounded by land and no surf or waves break on the shore, as they do where the beaches are unprotected. He says that when he was at the point or cape of Lapa he saw a very high island to the northeast, which would be some twenty-six leagues from him. He named it Belaforma, because from far away it must have seemed attractive. All of this is the mainland, but, as he moved about with the ships from one place to another within the gulf which was surrounded by land, bays were formed that created the appearance of separated lands, which the admiral called islands, because that is what he thought they were.

On Sunday the fifth of August, he sailed five leagues from the point of the cape of Lapa, which is the eastern cape of the Isla de Gracia. He saw very good harbors, one next to another, and he says that almost all of this sea is a harbor, because it is surrounded by islands and there are no waves. He called islands the regions created by inlets on the mainland, for only the island of Trinidad and the mainland surround this gulf, which he calls the sea. He sent the boats to shore and they found fish and fire and signs of people and a large house. From there he traveled eight leagues, where he found good harbors. He says this part of the Isla de Gracia has an extremely high coast and many valleys and all of it must be populated, he says, because he saw that it was completely cultivated. There are many rivers, because each valley has its own, league after league. They found many fruits, some like grapes, very flavorful, and very good mirabelles, and others like apples and others, he says, like oranges with insides like figs. They found an infinite number of wild cats. The waters, he says, are the best that they had seen. This island, he says, is filled with harbors. The seawater is fresh; not completely fresh everywhere, but brackish like that of Cartagena. He says that lower down it is fresh like the river in Seville. This was caused by the currents of seawater, which salted the river. . . .

The admiral could not get out of his mind the amount of fresh water that he had found and seen in the Golfo de la Ballena between the mainland and the island of Trinidad. And after thinking a great deal about it and sifting through his arguments, he came to believe that the earthly paradise must be in that region. One of the reasons that convinced him was the great temperateness that he observed in the land and sea where he was sailing, even though it was so close to the equator, which so many authors had judged to be inhabitable or habitable only with difficulty. Instead, during the mornings there, with the sun in the sign of Leo, it was so cool that he had to wrap himself in a cloak.

Another reason was that after traveling one hundred leagues from the Azores, from north to south in that region he found that the compass needles moved more than one quarter to the northwest. And as they went to the west the mild weather grew more calm and moderate, and he felt that the sea was rising and the ships were being lifted up gently to heaven. And he says the cause of this increase in altitude is the variability of the circle that the north star describes with the Guards.[8] The farther the ships go to the west, the more they are lifted, and they will rise higher and there will be more of a change in the stars and in the circles that they describe, he says. From this he arrived at the idea, against all the common knowledge of astrologers and philosophers, that the world was not round. That is, although the hemisphere that Ptolemy and the others knew about was round, this one, that they did not know about, was not round at all. Instead, he imagined it to be like half of a pear with a tall stem, or like a woman's nipple on a round ball, with this part of the stem higher in the air and closer to heaven and below the equator. And it appeared to him that the earthly paradise could be situated on that stem, even though it might be very far from where he currently was.

He gave another reason; he says he found the people to be whiter, or less black, with long, straight hair; they were more astute with greater intelligence, and were not cowardly. He gives an explanation of

---

[8]The Guards are the stars Beta and Gamma of Ursa Minor, farthest from the North Star; because they describe in a twenty-four hour period a complete circle around the polestar, observing their positions with respect to the North Star served to establish the time of night.

this: On this voyage, when he came to a latitude of twenty degrees, the people were black, and when he arrived at the Cape Verde Islands, they were more black, and when he came to five degrees, exactly on the latitude of the Sierra Leone, they were much more black; but when he turned toward the west and arrived at Trinidad and the mainland, which he believed to be the eastern extremity with respect to his location, the end of all of the land and the islands, he found great temperateness and serenity and, therefore, the people were just as he described them.

Another reason is the quantity and amount of fresh water in the Golfo de la Ballena, forty-eight leagues of it, which seems that it could have come from the spring of the terrestrial paradise, even though it might have come from very far away, and this gulf could be the source of the four rivers Nile, Tigris, Euphrates, and Ganges [Genesis 2.10–14], or it might flow into them through its cataracts below the earth and the sea.

It is certainly not surprising, considering that the world of the Indies had been so hidden and its discovery so recent, as well as the new things that he was seeing, that the admiral imagined so many different and new things and produced fantasies and a new theory.

19

ANDRÉS DEL CORRAL

Testimony concerning Columbus's Landing on the South American Mainland

Santo Domingo, June 16, 1512

As part of his efforts to regain all of the grants and titles originally ceded to his father, who had died in 1506, Diego Colón initiated in 1508 the first of a series of lawsuits against the Spanish crown that would go on for decades. The Darién case, in which Diego Colón sought, among other things, to establish exactly what lands Columbus had explored, was heard

William D. Phillips, Jr., ed., Mark D. Johnston, philologist, Anne Marie Wolf, trans., *Testimonies from the Columbian Lawsuits,* Repertorium Columbianum 8 (Turnhout, Belgium: Brepols, 2000), 49–56.

in Santo Domingo in 1512. The testimony, given by Columbus's page, Andrés del Corral, an eyewitness to the event, states that during his third voyage Columbus had indeed reached the South American mainland, although he himself had not actually gone ashore. Diego hoped that the establishment of this fact would legitimize his claim that his father had been the first European to reach the mainland of South America. The text is a summary transcript of the witness's testimony as recorded by the court clerk.

And the witnesses were presented on behalf of the admiral of the Indies in the lawsuit that he pursues with the attorney of the queen our lady about the government of the province of Darién, and the following questions were asked:

I. First, they should be asked if they know the parties.

II. Also, if they know and have knowledge of the provinces named Paria[1] and Urabá[2] and Darién[3] and Veragua.[4]

III. Also if they know, etc., that all the provinces are in the same land and sea coast.

IV. Also if they know that the admiral Sir Christopher Columbus discovered the province of Paria which is the beginning and the first of the provinces that in that land called the mainland was discovered before any Christian had gone to that land or had knowledge of it.

V. Also, if they know, etc., that the admiral on the later voyage that he made [the fourth voyage] discovered a land called Maya[5] where there was and is the point of Caxinas[6] and some islands of which one is called Guanaja,[7] and later he discovered through the land to the east until reaching Veragua, and he passed Veragua discovering toward the east.

VI. Also, if they know, etc., that it seemed to the people who sailed that later voyage with the admiral that they had discovered so far to the east in that land where Veragua is that Hispaniola already lay to the west, and when the admiral wanted to leave from there to Hispaniola they certainly thought that he was going to Castile, and they

---

[1] The Paria Peninsula, extending east from the northeast coast of Venezuela.
[2] A section of land adjacent to the Gulf of Urabá.
[3] Part of the Isthmus of Panama.
[4] Part of the Isthmus of Panama west of Darién.
[5] Possibly a reference to Honduras.
[6] Cape Honduras.
[7] Guanaja, or Bonacca, is one of the Islas de Bahía, lying off the Honduran coast.

became excited saying that they did not have good ships or supplies for it, thus, according to this, the admiral discovered to the east of Veragua at least two hundred leagues.

VII. Also, if they know, etc., that the province of Veragua is the westernmost of the provinces of the land called the mainland and the province that they call Paria is the easternmost in such a way that the provinces of Urabá and Darién lie between them in the same land.

VIII. Also, if they know, etc., that Their Highnesses made a grant to the admiral Sir Christopher Columbus of the offices of viceroy and governor in all the islands and mainland that he would discover or that would be discovered by his industry.

IX. Also, if they know or believe that what has been discovered in the land of Gracia that they call the mainland has been by the industry that the admiral expended in opening the door and making the first voyage in which he discovered the Indies, and in having thereafter first discovered the land they call the mainland that was Paria, from where those who thereafter have discovered and traveled along the coast began to follow until reaching Urabá and Darién, or to whatever part of it they reached.

X. Also, if they know that people who had sailed with the admiral on the first voyage later sailed on all the voyages of discovery in that land. The witnesses should say and declare the names of the persons and what they know about this.

XI. Also, if they know that the abovesaid and each thing about it has been common knowledge among those who went into and reached those parts and had knowledge of them.

And what each of the witnesses presented on behalf of the lord admiral Sir Diego Colón, viceroy and governor of these islands and mainland, having sworn in [legal] form and being asked about the questions of the interrogatory presented on behalf of the lord admiral, said and deposed about it is the following. . . .

Andrés del Corral, citizen of the town of Puerto Real, a witness presented on behalf of the admiral, having sworn and being asked the general questions and the questions of the interrogatory in which he was presented as a witness and to each of them and separately he said and deposed the following.

Asked the general questions, he said that this witness is about thirty-two or thirty-three years old. Asked if he is related by blood or marriage to any of the parties, he said no. Asked if he is a servant of anyone, he said he is a servant of the admiral Sir Diego Colón and was the same for the admiral his father. Asked if he has any hostility toward any of the parties, he said no. Asked if he were suborned, induced, influenced, corrupted, threatened, or advised by any of the parties or by anyone else, and if they had given or promised to give him anything so that he would say in his statement more or less than he knows, he said no. Asked if he wishes that one party would win unjustifiably in this lawsuit more than the other, he said no . . .

To the first question, he said that he knows the admiral Sir Diego Colón, because as he has said he lives with him and has known him for fourteen or fifteen years and that he does not know the royal attorney.

To the second question, he said that he knows the province of Paria contained in the question and that he does not know the other provinces. Asked how he knows the province of Paria, he said because he was there at the time that the admiral Sir Christopher Columbus discovered it.

To the third question, he said that he has heard it said that the provinces in the previous question are on the coast of the province of Paria and that everything is one coast. Asked from whom he heard it said, he said from the admiral and from other people whose names he does not recall.

To the fourth question, he said that he knows that the admiral Sir Christopher Columbus was the first who discovered the province of Paria. Asked how he knows it, he said because this witness came from Castile with the admiral as his page when he left from there with six ships, and he sent three of them to this island of Hispaniola, and he went with the other three on the route to discover and stopped at the province of Paria, where this witness saw how the admiral at the time that he discovered the province sent one Pedro de Terreros, his captain, ashore, and this witness and others went with him, and he saw that the people of that province were astonished at seeing the Christians, as people who had never seen them, and this witness never knew or heard it said that anyone before the admiral had discovered the province of Paria. And there in the name of the king and the queen, our lords, they took possession of the province which Pedro de Terreros took by command of the admiral because he did not go ashore then because his eyes were ailing, and also this witness said that he believes it because before the province of Paria was discovered the mariners who sailed with the admiral said to him that they should return to Hispaniola, saying that they would not find land there and the admiral did not wish [to return] until he discovered the province. . . .

To the seventh question, he said that he has heard what is contained in the question. Asked by what people he heard it said, he said by the adelantado Sir Bartolomé Colón and by Ojeda[8] and by other people who know the sailing chart whose names he does not recall.

To the eighth question, he said that he knows it because he has seen the privileges.

To the ninth question, he said that he knows it. Asked how he knows it, he knows it because of what he said in the previous question and because it is well known that in our times no person had passed or discovered these parts until the admiral Sir Christopher discovered them, and that this witness, being in the court in Madrid with the admiral at the time that he negotiated the voyage of discovery with Their Highnesses, the admiral, seeing how the council members and many others were opposed to him, said to Their Highnesses that because they did not believe him, he would give them a person whom they would believe, and that then a friar of the order of St. Francis arrived, whose name he does not know, who said to Their Highnesses that what the admiral said was true, and then they sent him and he came to these parts to discover, and that because of this he believes and knows what he has said and what is contained in the question.

To the tenth question, he said that he has heard it said that some of the mariners who had first gone with the admiral went to discover with Ojeda. Asked by whom he heard it said, he said that he does not remember.

To the eleventh question, he said that what he has said is common knowledge among people who know about it and that it is the truth by the oath that he swore and he signed it with his name, and he was not asked the other questions because he was not presented for the other questions.

[8]Alonso de Ojeda (1466–ca. 1515), a ship's captain who accompanied Columbus on his second voyage. In 1499 he received permission from Juan Rodríguez de Fonseca to make voyages of discovery and exploration independently of Columbus.

20

CHRISTOPHER COLUMBUS

Letter to Juana de la Torre, Making the Case for the Restitution of His Privileges

Late 1500

After exploring the coast of Venezuela, Columbus sailed to Hispaniola, where he resumed his functions as governor but was unable to control the chaotic situation there. He was removed from his governorship and sent back to Spain under arrest in October 1500. During this period he composed this self-justificatory letter to Juana de la Torre, the mistress of the household of Prince Juan of Spain. Presenting a very personal view of the events that had taken place on Hispaniola, Columbus accuses the colonists of disobedience and the monarchs of disloyalty, charges the royal commissioner Francisco de Bobadilla with lying, and describes his own motivations.

Transcript of an open letter that the admiral wrote to the governess of Prince Juan (may he be in glory), in the year 1500, while he was returning from the Indies under arrest.

Most honorable lady. If my complaint about the world is new, its habit of mistreatment is very ancient. A thousand battles I have fought, resisting them all until now when neither arms nor intelligence have availed me. With cruelty it has cast me into darkness. Faith in the creator of all men sustains me, however; his help has always been very ready. Once, not long ago, when I was feeling overwhelmed, with his right arm he raised me up, saying: "O man of little faith, rise, for I am; do not be afraid." I came with such sincere love to serve these princes and have performed services the likes of which have never been heard of or seen before.

Of the new heaven and earth that our Lord made, as St. John writes in the Apocalypse, after having spoken through the mouth of Isaiah, I

Helen Nader, ed. and trans., Luciano Formisano, ed., *The Book of Privileges Issued to Christopher Columbus by King Fernando and Queen Isabel 1492–1502,* Repertorium Columbianum 2 (Berkeley: University of California Press, 1996), 161–69.

was made the messenger and showed the place.[1] All were incredulous except the queen, my lady, whose intelligent spirit and great strength prevailed, making her heiress of all as a dear and most beloved daughter. The possession of all this I went to take in her royal name. Everyone sought to make amends for their ignorance by overlooking their own little knowledge by speaking of impediments and costs. Her Highness approved it, nonetheless, and supported it as much as she could.

Seven years passed in discussions and nine in the execution, during which many notable and memorable things occurred that no one had foreseen at all. I have arrived and continue in such a condition that there is no one so vile that he does not think of insulting me. Virtue, however, will reward in this world those who do not consent to this. If I were to steal the Indies or the land that lies in their vicinity, which everyone is talking about now, from Christendom and give it to the Muslims, I could not be shown greater enmity in Spain. Who would believe such a thing where there was always such magnanimity? I would have abandoned this business had it been fair to the queen, but the strength of our Lord and of Her Highness urged me to persevere. In order to relieve the queen somewhat of the suffering that death [of Prince Juan on October 4, 1497] was inflicting on her then, I undertook a fresh voyage to the new heaven and world that had remained concealed until then. If this voyage is not held in such high esteem there as others to the Indies, it is no wonder, because it seemed to come about as a result of my expertise. The Holy Spirit inflamed St. Peter, and with him another twelve who all fought here. Their efforts and troubles were many, yet finally they won a victory over all.

I believed that this voyage to Paria would pacify the situation somewhat, what with the pearls there and the gold strike on Hispaniola. I ordered the people to collect and fish for pearls, and agreed with them that I would return and pay them at the rate of one-half *fanega*. If I did not write about this to Their Highnesses, it was because I first wanted to arrange the same with the gold. This turned out for me just like a lot of other things. I would not have lost them or my honor if I had looked out for my own good and allowed Hispaniola to be lost, or if my own privileges and agreements were observed. Likewise, I say the same about the gold that I had collected because, with the many resulting deaths and labors, only by divine virtue could the business

[1]An allusion to the continent of Paria (South America).

have been brought to perfection. When I left Paria [and sailed to Hispaniola], I found almost half of the people on the island in rebellion. They have fought me as if I were a Muslim up to now, while the Indians have harassed me seriously on the other flank. Then Ojeda came and tried to seal my fate. He said that Their Highnesses were sending him with promises of gifts, exemptions, and pay. He attracted a great following, for on the whole of Hispaniola there are few except vagrants, and none with a wife and children. This Ojeda harassed me greatly. When it was necessary for him to go, he left saying that he would return soon with more ships and people, and worse, that when he had left Spain, the royal person of the queen, our lady, was near death. . . .

For six months I had been ready for the return trip to Their Highnesses with the good news about the gold and eager to flee from governing dissolute people who do not fear God or the king and queen and are full of defiance and malice. I only needed 600,000 *maravedís* to pay the people, and for this there were four million and some more from tithes after discounting the royal third from the gold. Many times before my departure I asked Their Highnesses to send someone there at my cost to take charge of justice. After I found the judge in rebellion, I again asked Their Highnesses for some staff, or at least a servant, with letters, because my fame is such that, were I to build churches and hospitals, these would be known as dens for thieves. Finally, when they appointed someone [Francisco de Bobadilla], it was exactly the opposite of what the business required. May it succeed because it was done at their specifications. . . .

The day after he arrived, Bobadilla created himself interim governor, appointed officials, pronounced sentences, and announced exemptions from gold restrictions, tithes, and all other things in general for twenty years, which, as I say, is a generation. He also announced that he would pay everyone, even though they may not have served fully until that day. Furthermore, he gave notice that he planned to send me and my brothers back to Spain in irons, as he did, and that I could never return there, and neither could anyone of my lineage, saying a thousand dishonest and discourteous things about me.

All this occurred the day after he arrived, as I said, while I was absent far away and unaware of him or his arrival. . . .

It would be good if the Indies were settled by honorable people from Castile whose identities and professions are known. I had agreed with the citizens' request that they pay one-third of the gold and the tithes. They accepted this as a favor from Their Highnesses. I reprimanded them, however, when I heard that they were not paying it. I expected that the commander would do likewise, but he did the contrary. He turned them against me by saying that I wanted to deprive them of what Their Highnesses had given them. He tried to get them to turn their backs on me, which he did, and then he persuaded them to write to Their Highnesses asking them never again to make me responsible for the island's governance. Furthermore, he ordered investigations of me and my brothers for misdeeds, the likes of which have never been heard of in hell. I trust in our Lord, who rescued Daniel and the three boys [cf. Book of Daniel, ch. 3] with such knowledge, force, and disposition as he had, if it should please him and be his desire. . . .

Bobadilla made it his first order of business to seize the gold, which had not been measured or weighed yet. In my absence, he said that he would pay the people from it. According to what I heard, he paid himself first and then sent new procurers to collect ore in the mines. Of this gold I had set aside certain samples, enormous nuggets, like the eggs of geese, hens, pullets, and of many other shapes, which some individuals had gathered in a short time. These would have pleased Their Highnesses and helped them to comprehend the business when they received a quantity of large stones full of gold. He pocketed this for himself first thing so that Their Highnesses would not highly regard this business before he feathered his own nest, which he is in great haste to do. The gold that was ready for smelting disappeared at the fire, while some chains that weighed up to twenty marks have never been seen again! I have been greatly harmed in this matter of the gold, even more so than with the pearls, for not having brought it to Their Highnesses.

The commander soon put into effect everything that he thought could hurt me. As I have already said, with 600,000 *maravedís* I could pay everyone without robbing anyone, and I had collected more than four million in tithes and fees without counting the gold. He made some very generous gifts that are outrageous, though I think he began by giving himself the first share. Their Highnesses will find out about it there when they order his audit, especially if I am in on it. He does nothing but say that a great sum is owed. In fact, that is just what I have said and probably not as much. I have been greatly distressed in having an investigator sent with authority over me who knows that, if the judicial report that he sends back is very negative, he will probably remain there as governor. . . .

I know that my errors have not been done for evil purposes, and I think that Their Highnesses will believe the same as I have said, and I know and see that they deal mercifully with those who maliciously do them disservice. Therefore, I believe and hold most certain that their compassion will be much better and abundant toward me, who [am their creature] and fell into disservice through ignorance and under duress, as they will learn in full later. They will look at my services and recognize more and more that they have benefited greatly. Everything will be weighed in the balance, just as the holy scripture tells us, the good together with the bad on the day of judgment. If they still insist that another person should judge me, which I do not expect, and that it should be by audit of the Indies, I very humbly beg them to send there two individuals of conscience and honor, at my expense. I think these will easily discover that five marks of gold can be found in four hours. In either case, it is very important that they provide for this matter.

The commander, on arriving at Santo Domingo, lodged in my house just as he found it. He appropriated everything as his own. He is welcome, because perhaps he needed it (although no pirate ever did this to a merchant!). I have a major complaint about my documents. They have been taken from me, and not one of them has been retrieved from him. Those that would have benefited me the most in my acquittal are the ones he has best kept concealed. Behold the just and honest inspector he is! They tell me that all the many things that he may have done are within the letter of the law, if not its spirit. God our Lord is present with his forces and knowledge, as always, and in the end punishes ingratitude resulting from injuries in each instance.

Fourth Voyage, 1502–1504

21

Writ Ordering Restitution of Property to the Admiral and His Brothers

Granada, September 27, 1501

This writ, issued by Fernando and Isabel prior to the admiral's fourth voyage to the Indies, restores to Columbus and his brothers the property that had been confiscated from them by Francisco de Bobadilla, who on September 3, 1501, had been replaced as governor of Hispaniola by Nicolás de Ovando. The writ appoints Alonso Sánchez de Carvajal, who had been a member of Queen Isabel's staff, royal provisioner of the second voyage, and commander of a ship on the third, to be Columbus's representative in the Indies.

The King and the Queen. We decree and order that the following must be done in matters of property pertaining to Sir Christopher Columbus, our admiral of the Ocean Sea. First, regarding his contribution of one-eighth of the merchandise that we order sent to the islands and mainland now and in the future, should the admiral put up one-eighth of such merchandise or its equivalent, then after deducting the costs and expenses, he shall keep for himself one-eighth of the profits obtained from this merchandise, in accord with the stipulations of the capitulation made with him about this.

Commander Bobadilla took for himself some gold, jewels, and other movable, semi-movable, and real property that the admiral had on the island of Hispaniola. Because those comprised the product and revenue of these Indies, we order that above all else the admiral shall be reimbursed costs, expenditures, and wages that were owed during

Helen Nader, ed. and trans., Luciano Formisano, ed., *The Book of Privileges Issued to Christopher Columbus by King Fernando and Queen Isabel 1492–1502*, Repertorium Columbianum 2 (Berkeley: University of California Press, 1996), 180–82.

the time that the admiral last went to the Indies in the year ninety-eight, counting from the time he arrived on the island of Hispaniola, and should have been paid from these things that were taken from him. Although financial responsibility for the Indies belongs to the admiral according to the capitulation, nevertheless it was understood that these expenses should be paid from what was acquired from the Indies. Whatever remains after having paid all these expenses should be divided into ten shares, of which nine will be for us and the tenth for the admiral. From these nine-tenths we agreed to pay the wages, costs, and expenses until that voyage when the admiral went to the island of Hispaniola in the year ninety-eight, because we granted him exemption from his share of those expenses. The admiral shall pay from his one-tenth what it has been verified that he owes personally to some people as admiral.

Concerning the livestock that have been sent from there, according to the capitulation, the costs and expenses for this were to be at our cost, while the admiral was to have one-tenth of what remains. In consideration of this, it is our pleasure to order that he shall be credited with one-tenth of the gross of these livestock and any calves they have produced. The remaining nine-tenths belong to us.

We order that all his personal and household furnishings and supplies of bread and wine that Commander Bobadilla took from him, or their fair equivalent, shall be returned and restored to him without our taking any portion of it at all. Among other things that Commander Bobadilla took from the admiral was a certain quantity of stones from the gold field that contained some gold. We order our governor [Friar Nicolás de Ovando] of these islands to take a sworn statement from Commander Bobadilla about how many and what sizes they were and make him restore them so that they can be divided and distributed in the stated manner.

We order that the admiral should receive restitution for two mares with their colts, which the admiral bought from a farmer in the Indies, and two horses that the admiral owned: one that he bought from Gorbalán,[1] and the other that he had from the mares that Commander Bobadilla took from him, or their fair equivalent, without our receiving any portion of this at all.

The admiral says that he was harmed by not being permitted to appoint the captains and officers of the ships that we are ordering to go to the island of Hispaniola, which he claims he should have ap-

---

[1] Ginés de Gorbalán, captain of one of the ships on Columbus's second voyage.

pointed according to the capitulation. Although the present captains and officers have already been appointed by our order, we say that in the future we will order that they be appointed in accord with the capitulation.

We declare and order that from now on the admiral can take from the island of Hispaniola 111 hundredweights of brazilwood representing his one-tenth that he is entitled to have from the 1,000 hundredweights of brazilwood that by our command are to be given yearly to the merchants with whom a contract has been signed. By our contract with these merchants, their share is exempted from what the admiral is to receive during the term contracted with the merchants and afterwards the one-tenth shall be reserved for the admiral.

The admiral claims that Commander Bobadilla has paid some back wages and other things on the island of Hispaniola to some persons who were not owed wages or anything else, as may be seen in the books of the officials and can be proved and demonstrated. We order that, although the commander made payments to persons not owed wages or anything else, the admiral is not obligated to continue paying them.

Commander Bobadilla took from the admiral's brothers a certain quantity of gold and jewels that had accrued to them by virtue of governing the Indies. All of this shall be divided into ten shares, of which the admiral shall receive one, while the remaining nine shares belong to us. As for the furnishings, supplies, fields, and houses that the Columbus brothers had, and the gold received from having sold their things, if it is proved that this was the case, and although we have the right to some of this, we give it all to the Columbus brothers as a favor so that they may dispose of it as their own private property.

It is our wish and command that the admiral have on the island of Hispaniola someone in charge of his treasury to receive what he is supposed to have; This person shall be Alonso Sánchez de Carvajal, of our household staff. On behalf of the admiral, Alonso Sánchez de Carvajal shall be present with our auditor to watch the smelting and stamping of the gold that is acquired on the islands and mainland. He and our agent shall be responsible for buying and selling this merchandise. We order our governor, accountant, judges, and officials who now and in the future may be on the islands and mainland, to implement and enforce all of this according to our wish and command. Alonso Sánchez de Carvajal shall supply whoever displays the proper power of attorney from the admiral with that portion of the gold that belongs to him in payment of the one-tenth of the island, net, as well as the one-eighth of the profit from merchandise whose cost he demonstrates that the admiral financed.

The admiral had subcontracted the offices of sheriff and clerk for the island of Hispaniola for a specific time. We order that the cash and whatever revenues and value these offices have generated shall be divided into ten shares, after first having paid the costs and expenses of these officials: nine shares shall be for us and one share for the admiral. Whoever received the office of clerk was not obligated to pay a fixed price for it. We order that whenever he wishes to leave this office he should appear with all he has acquired, so that it can be divided in this way. The books and documents that were taken from him shall be returned to him. If any of them are needed for business, a transcript certified by a public clerk shall be copied and the originals returned to him.

Concerning the lease and supplies, Carvajal shall profit from all of it according to and as our other officials do. We order you, our governor, accountant, and other officials, judges, and personnel of the islands and mainland to do and implement all and every part of this as stipulated. In implementing it, give and turn over to the admiral, his brothers, and his representative these things without creating any impediment or doing the contrary.

Done in Granada on the twenty-seventh day of September in the year one thousand five hundred and one. I, the King. I, the Queen. By order of the king and queen. Gaspar de Gricio.[2]

---

[2]Gaspar de Gricio (d. 1506 or 1507) appears as royal secretary as early as March 1476.

22

BARTOLOMÉ DE LAS CASAS

On Columbus's Fourth Voyage

ca. 1527–1563

This selection picks up the story from Columbus's arrival off Hispaniola in July 1502. He had sailed from Spain with four ships on May 9, 1502, with orders to explore the western Caribbean and search for a possible passage to the East Indies. Off the coast of Hispaniola his ships encountered a hurricane, which destroyed a large Spanish fleet that was homeward bound from Hispaniola. This excerpt is taken from Las Casas's History; *it both paraphrases and records Columbus's observations on the voyage.*

ARRIVAL AT HISPANIOLA, 14 JULY 1502–23 JUNE 1503

We recounted how the admiral left from close by this harbor at Santo Domingo to shelter from the great storm he had predicted and how he and his four ships rode out the danger and peril involved in that storm and came eventually to Puerto Hermoso or Puerto Escondido. From there he headed west, putting in at the harbor at Yaquimo, or as he called it Puerto del Brasil, some eighty leagues from Santo Domingo.

When he left there on 14 July 1502, his plan was to make for the mainland but he found himself becalmed for a lengthy spell from lack of wind. He managed to approach a number of the small islands close to Jamaica where, even though there is no fresh surface water, it proved possible to get enough fresh water for the four ships by digging a number of boreholes near the sea's edge. The lack of wind became even more acute and he found himself drifting in the current towards the many islands off Cuba which he had christened, when he first discovered both them and Cuba in 1495,[1] Jardín de la Reina. From there, with favorable winds, he headed for the mainland only to encounter contrary winds and strong currents which he could do

---

[1] Actually 1494.

Nigel Griffin, ed. and trans., *Las Casas on Columbus: Background and the Second and Fourth Voyages,* Repertorium Columbianum 7 (Turnhout, Belgium: Brepols 1999), 193–240.

nothing to resist. He spent the next sixty days contending with violent storms, downpours, thunder and lightning, without even a glimpse of the stars, and it seemed as though the whole world were falling in on itself. In all that time, he managed only sixty leagues. What with the violence of the original storm and all the battling against wind and current and the violent buffeting and shaking they endured, all the ships were holed; almost all those on board fell ill from lack of sleep and the exertions to which they were exposed, and the admiral himself, in a perpetual state of anxiety and sleeplessness, was so poorly that he was on the brink of death. Eventually, after experiencing enormous hardships and being exposed to extremes of peril and unspeakable labors, they reached a small unknown island, known as Guanaja to the Indians and surrounded by three or four smaller islands which the Spaniards later named the Guanajas. All these islands were thickly inhabited.

Here the admiral ordered his brother, the adelantado [Bartolomé Colón], captain of one of the ships, to go ashore to learn what he could. He took two ship's boats crammed with men and found the inhabitants to be peace loving and with all the characteristics of those who dwell in the islands in this part of the world, save that they did not have the broad foreheads that are so typical. Because the island was covered in pine trees, the admiral named it Isla de Pinos.[2] The island lay some twelve leagues from the point known today as Honduras where the Spaniards built the city known then and now as Trujillo and where today a mere five or six people still live. . . .

The adelantado put ashore on this island of Guanaja or the Guanajas[3] and found himself approached by a canoe full of Indians. As long as a galley and some eight foot wide, it was laden with merchandise from the west and must indeed have come from the land of Yucatán which lies some thirty leagues or a shade further off to the west. The central part of the canoe was covered with a matting awning fashioned from palm leaves of the kind known in New Spain as *petates,* and inside, beneath this awning, were the women and children and household effects and the merchandise itself, kept completely dry from both rain and seawater. The merchandise and other goods they carried consisted of many cotton cloaks, in a variety of colors and patterns, sleeveless blouses, also painted and embroidered, and cloths, identi-

---

[2]There is a confusion here: Isla de Pinos lies off the coast of Cuba, whereas Guanaja, or Bonacca, lies off the coast of Honduras in the Islas de Bahía.

[3]The Islas de Bahía, off the coast of Honduras.

cally colored and patterned, of the kind their menfolk use to wrap round their privy parts. They also had wooden swords, with slots running along the edges of the blade into which pieces of sharp flint had been set, with pitch and twine; also copper axes with which to chop fuelwood, and gourds and some patens or crucibles for melting copper. They also carried many cacao kernels of the kind used in New Spain, Yucatán, and other places as currency. They lived off maize bread and certain edible roots which must have been what we here on Hispaniola call sweet potatoes and are known in New Spain as *camotes*. Their wine was also made from maize and tasted like beer....

As he made his way around this region, the admiral still persisted in his belief that he might obtain news of Cathay and the Grand Khan, and he took these cloaks and brightly painted goods to be a sign that he had begun to make contact with that world he was anxious to explore. When the Indians saw how insistent he was on finding out where there might be gold, they proceeded to regale him with endless stories to the effect that there was a great deal of gold in this land or in that, and that they knew of a place further inland, in the direction of Cathay, where the people wore circlets of gold on their heads, sported thick gold bands round their wrists and ankles, and had embroidered cloaks and chairs and tables and chests encrusted with gold. He showed them coral whenever he could and the Indians told him that they knew where women wore strings of coral round their heads that hung down their backs. He showed them peppers and other spices and received a reply that they knew a place where such things were plentiful. The more he showed them things the more the Indians readily agreed that they knew where they were available simply because they saw that to say so gave such pleasure, even when they had never before seen or even heard of the things they were showing them and he was inquiring about. They went further, even claiming that the people who lived in the lands of which they spoke had ships and cannons, bows and arrows, swords and cuirasses,[4] and anything else they saw the Christians had. The admiral even fancied they were telling him that there were horses, which was something they had never seen and the admiral did not have with him at the time. They informed him that across the sea lay Ciguare, which he assumed was some city or province in the kingdoms of the Grand Khan, and that from there it was only ten days' journey to the river Ganges. And

---

[4]Armor for the upper body, consisting of a breastplate and backplate.

when they indicated to him that one of the provinces which was rich in gold was Veragua, the admiral supposed that the lands concerned lay at the other end of the channel from Veragua, as Tortosa does from Fuenterrabía, almost as if one was on the coast of one sea and the other on the coast of another. It seems that the admiral divined the existence of another ocean, the one we today know as the Southern Ocean, and of course he was right about this, even though he was wrong about all the rest of it. All of this came about because the whole conversation was conducted in sign language, and either the Indians were deliberately playing games with him or he simply understood nothing of what they were trying to say and only heard what he wanted to hear. He drew up a detailed report on all these matters for the king and queen during the time he spent marooned, as we shall see, on Jamaica, and I have a copy of his report in front of me. . . .

Eventually, on the feast of Epiphany [January 6] of 1503, they sailed into a river, known to the Indians as Yebra and which the admiral christened Belén [Bethlehem] in memory of the arrival on that day of the three Magi in the holy place. A league or two beyond this river lies another, known in the Indian language as Veragua.[5] The admiral ordered that soundings be taken at the mouth of the first (which is done by taking the lead and seeing how many hands and cubits deep the water is) and then in the mouth of the second, and the findings were that there were fourteen hands of clear water at high tide in the mouth of the Belén and that the Veragua was much shallower. The ships' boats made their way up the Belén until they reached the settlement where they had been informed the Veragua gold mines were located, but the local inhabitants lined up, with their weapons, to bar their way and prevent their landing, and would not converse with them or listen to what the Spaniards had to say.

The next day the boats made their way up the Veragua only to find the local people there behaving in exactly the same way, calling each other to arms. Not only did they try to prevent the men from landing but they also attacked them while they were still in the boats. However, the Spaniards had with them an Indian from that coastal region and he understood their language and managed to calm them down, explaining that these were good people who did not intend to take anything from them without paying for it first, and with that assurance they started to barter and trade with the Christians. They acquired up to twenty gold mirrors and a number of tubes of gold dust and grains

[5] In present-day Panama.

of gold to smelt. In order to raise the price of their gold, these Indians pretended they had to travel a long way to get it, up into a very rocky mountain range, and that when they went prospecting they had to go without food and leave behind their womenfolk and other similar comforts.

Having established that there was more clearance to get the ships up the river Belén, the admiral decided to do so and on Monday the ninth of January two ships entered the river, the other two waiting for high tide on the next day before following suit because they drew more, even though the difference there between the depth at high and low tide was never more than two hands.

The Indians came down straight away to trade what they had with the Christians, and most of what they had to offer was fish, for so many fish swim up that river at certain times of the year that no one who had not seen it for himself would ever believe it. They also had gold which they traded for pins, and anything more valuable or which they possessed in greater quantity they exchanged for beads and hawk's bells. Since all the Indians they had consulted had indicated how important and rich the gold mines were in Veragua, the adelantado went out to sea again in the ships' boats, three days after entering the river Belén, with the intention of making his way up the river Veragua as far as the town where the king of the country lived whose name was Quibia. Learning of the arrival of the Christians, this king and his people got into their canoes and paddled downriver to welcome them. When the canoes and the boats met up, they welcomed the Christians very warmly, as though they were brothers. The king presented the adelantado with some of the gold jewelry he was wearing and the adelantado returned the compliment with trinkets and barter goods from Castile, both parties being very happy with the exchange and parting on very friendly terms. The king then returned to his town in the canoes and the adelantado took his boats back to the ships.

The next day the king came out to the ships to meet the admiral and, since they had little to talk about because neither understood the language of the other, it was little more than an hour before the admiral presented him with some things from Castile and the men traded some gold jewelry in return for hawk's bells, and the two parted company without much by way of ceremony, the king returning whence he had come. The Spaniards were now feeling rested and secure when, on the twenty-fourth of January which was a Tuesday, there was a sudden flash flood in the river Belén and, before anything could be done to anchor the ships more firmly, the wall of water smashed into the admiral's flagship with such force that one of the two anchors broke and she was flung violently into one of the other ships, snapping her bonaventure mizzen, which is one of the masts which carries a certain type of sail, and the two vessels, dragging their anchors, then proceeded to stagger from one side of the river to the other, smashing against each other time and again as they did so, and it was a miracle that all four ships were not lost as a result. This sudden flash flood must have been caused by a downpour high up in the mountains above Veragua, such downpours being common here in the Indies. . . .

Once these difficult days were over with their bad weather and great worry for everyone and especially for the admiral, the sea became calm and on Monday the sixth of February he sent the commander by sea with sixty-eight men as far as the mouth of the Veragua, a league or so off to the west, and they then made their way upriver for a further league and a half until they came to the town of the king we mentioned earlier called Quibia, and there they spent a day inquiring about how to get to the mines. They then traveled a further four and a half leagues before spending the night near a river which they had to ford forty-three times before they reached the mines accompanied by three Indians whom this king had sent with them to act as guides.

The admiral records, in the letter he wrote to the king and queen when he was on Jamaica, how the guides showed them a number of places in the area where gold could be found in quantity. Within two hours of their arrival, every one of the Spaniards had found his own little hoard of gold by scrabbling between the roots of the trees (for the whole area is thickly wooded) and, as a result, when they made it back that day as far as the town and the following day to the ships themselves, they were all very happy because they were persuaded that, if they could find so much gold in such a short space of time and with no labor whatever, it normally taking such an effort to extract the ore, it was a clear indication, albeit that their total haul did not amount to very much, that the region must be very rich indeed in gold. It later became clear that these mines were not those of Veragua, which were closer by, but rather those of Urirá, a town belonging to enemies of Veragua whither the king had apparently decided to direct the Spaniards in order to annoy his enemies and also, according to Sir Fernando,[6] in the hope that they would be taken with the idea of going there and leave his country alone.

---

[6]Columbus's son, who was with him on this voyage.

The admiral once again sent the adelantado [Bartolomé Colón] ashore to explore the coastal area to the west and also inland and discover the nature of the country. The commander left on Thursday the sixteenth of February of this same year 1503, with fifty men as well as one of the ship's boats which was carrying a further fourteen. The boats came the next day to the mouth of a river named Urirá, six or seven leagues to the west of Belén. When the local chief learned that they were coming, he and up to twenty of his men came out of their town a league in order to welcome them, presenting them with a great deal of food and supplies and bartering some gold mirrors. After a short time there on the spot where they met, both Indians and Christians made their way to the town where a great crowd came out to greet them. They had made ready a large house for their use and there they were accommodated and presented with a wide variety of foods to eat. It was not long before they received a visit from another local leader, the chief of Dururi, and a large group of his men, and they brought some gold mirrors to barter. From the locals and the visitors from Dururi they learned that there were quite a number of chiefs further inland who had large hoards of gold and carried weapons like we do, though it later transpired that either the Indians were lying because they did not want the Spaniards going any further inland or the Spaniards had not understood what they were trying to convey by signs. As for the first statement, that they had a great deal of gold, that was perfectly true, as Pedrárias's men discovered later when they made their way overland to the Southern Ocean.[7]

Next day the adelantado sent some of the men back overland to the ships, since he now knew how good and gentle the Indians were and how welcoming and kind they were to Christians. Taking with him just thirty men to explore further inland, he made his way to a town called Cobrava where there were more than six leagues of maize plantations and from there he continued on to another known as Cateba. In both places he and his men were very well received and given a great deal to eat and allowed to acquire some gold mirrors by bartering. These mirrors were like the patens that accompany a chalice, some large in size, others smaller, and they weighed around twelve ducats, some more some less. The Indians wore them around their necks on a thread of cotton, just as we wear an *agnus dei*.[8] Since the adelantado had by now gone a considerable distance from the ships

[7]In 1513 Pedro Arias de Ávila (ca. 1440–1530) led an expedition to present-day Panama.

[8]A small religious medal stamped with the figure of a lamb, honoring "the lamb of God."

and had found no harbor along that coast and shoreline any deeper than the one at Belén, he and his men made their way back the way they had come, taking with them a great deal of gold that they had obtained from the Indians by bartering for it. He received a very warm welcome from his brother, the admiral, since he was the bearer not only of good tidings but also of clear evidence of just how rich that country was in gold. Delighted to have evidence of just how promising this country was, and how rich it was and indeed still is, the admiral was buoyed up with optimism and decided to leave his brother, the adelantado [Bartolomé Colón], there with the main force of the Spaniards to build a settlement and subjugate the country, while he himself returned to Spain to obtain fresh supplies and more recruits. . . .

MAROONED ON JAMAICA, 23 JUNE 1503–JULY 1504

They then set out in search of the island of Jamaica since the prevailing winds and currents made it impossible for them to head for Hispaniola. The ships were holed so badly that they were on the point of sinking and, no matter how hard the men worked at the three pumps each vessel carried, the water level kept on rising and in one ship it all but reached the deck. The eve of St. John's Day saw them make harbor on Jamaica, at a place called Puerto Bueno and, although it offered them effective shelter against a storm, there was nothing there to assuage their hunger or slake their thirst, for there was no fresh water nor any Indian settlement.

After spending the feast of St. John [June 24] in this harbor, they then set off for another, called Santa Gloria,[9] still having to work flat out because their vessels were still in the same parlous state. When they reached this harbor, they realized the ships could go no further and so they ran them ashore close together as far as they could, which was more or less a crossbow shot from the shoreline, and then, using ropes, made them fast there side by side so that they would not budge. Even then, the water rose almost to the decks at high tide and they had to fashion sleeping quarters for the men in the fore and sterncastles.

When they had made their ships safe in this fashion and turned them into a place to stay, they were visited by Indians in canoes who came to trade their things and also supplies in exchange for goods from Castile. . . .

The admiral started to discuss with his leading men just how they might escape from this prison and get at least as far as Hispaniola.

[9]St. Ann's Bay.

They found themselves without practically any of the usual avenues of escape: it was no use waiting there in the hope that some vessel might arrive by chance—that would only happen if the Lord was to stage a miracle—and they were short of everything required for building new ships, above all craftsmen with the necessary skills. After many days spent discussing over and over again the pros and cons of various courses of action, and rehearsing the dangers involved in each and the possible solutions, they reached the conclusion, which the admiral embraced, that they must find a way to inform the commander-in-chief and governor of Hispaniola and also the admiral's own factor on the island that he and his men were marooned there on Jamaica and ask them to send out one of the vessels available laden with food and other vital supplies purchased out of the admiral's income on the island. For this mission he appointed two men in whose courage, good sense, and loyalty he had complete confidence, it being no simple task to cross such a large stretch of water in canoes made out of a single tree trunk, the distance from the very tip of Jamaica to the closest point on Hispaniola being twenty-five leagues, to which one has to add a further thirty-five from where they were to the easternmost point on Jamaica. These men would need to be resolute, determined, knowledgeable, and loyal if they were to accomplish the whole of this task successfully.

There is only one small island in the whole of this gulf, a rock known as Navasa eight leagues from this island of Hispaniola. Getting from Jamaica to Navasa was an undertaking requiring great courage and nobility of spirit because these canoes are about as unstable as a calabash [a gourd], consisting as they do of a single hollowed tree-trunk which, once in the water, sits little more than a hand's breadth above the surface. The Indians are not so much at risk in such canoes because, when they turn over, they simply swim back and bale out the canoe with gourds and then get back in, since the canoe itself does not sink but, being a piece of wood, simply floats on the surface of the water. The men chosen were a certain Diego Méndez de Segura, who had come out with the fleet as chief clerk and whom I got to know personally, a man of honor and of sound sense as well as being very well spoken, and one Bartolomeo Fieschi, a Genoese, also a good choice for such an important mission.[10]

Each man had his own canoe and was joined by six Spaniards as crew plus ten Indians to do the paddling. Diego Méndez was instructed,

---

[10]Bartolomeo Fieschi (ca. 1470–ca. 1530), a captain on Columbus's fourth voyage, ended up in Spain and was with Columbus when he died in 1506.

after reaching Santo Domingo, to carry on to Castile to present the king and queen with letters from the admiral describing his voyage, while Bartolomeo Fieschi was to go ashore on Hispaniola and then return to Jamaica to let him know that Diego Méndez had left and gone on ahead. The distance from the spot where the admiral and his men were stranded to this city of Santo Domingo was a good two hundred leagues. He wrote a long letter to the king and queen, a copy of which sits before me as I write, and in it he gave a detailed account of his voyage and of the sorrows, labors, and dangers he had passed and great adversities that had befallen him, the land he had discovered for the first time, and the rich mines at Veragua, and once again catalogued the great service he had done their majesties in the discovery of this new world and the labors he had endured in the process. . . .

The admiral wrote also the commander-in-chief who was governor here on the island, informing him about the desperate situation he was in and recommending to him the two men carrying his message, asking that he approve their departure and look kindly upon the dispatch of a vessel to assist him, and also that he give his permission for him and those still with him to land on Hispaniola. He then gave these letters and other documents intended for Castile to Diego Méndez and Bartolomeo Fieschi and saw them off in the two canoes, together with the Indians, each with his calabash full of water, some roots, and some cassava bread, and the Spaniards with their swords, shields, and as much by way of provisions — water, bread, and hutia or rabbit meat — as the canoe could carry, which was not all that much. It was vital that, once they got to the very tip of the island of Jamaica, some thirty leagues from where the admiral was stranded, and before they set out across such a vast stretch of rough water (for the sea is always rough in this ocean, especially between islands) in what was for us such a fragile kind of craft — though for the Indians, as we have said, to do so was less dangerous than it is for one of us to sail in a large ship — they should wait for the sea to become particularly calm. Then they could begin the crossing. The adelantado traveled on foot with a band of men to this same end of the island to ensure that the Indians in that area did nothing to prevent the canoes from leaving or damage them in any way. He would then make his way slowly back to the ships, stopping in each of the Indian townships and ensuring that good relations were established with them all.

After the two canoes had waited in this way at the eastern end or tip of the island of Jamaica, the sea did indeed become particularly calm. So, by night, and entrusting themselves to the Lord, they took their leave of the commander and set out with the sinews of the ten Indian volunteers doing all the work. These Indians were anxious to assist them in their plight in any way they could, even, as will become clear, risking their lives in the process. The calm weather persisted all night and all the next day and they made progress, with the Indians working hard at the sticks that serve them as paddles. The heat was intense and they had only a little water on board to keep themselves cool and so, from time to time, the Indians would take a dip in the sea. They ate while they paddled and so made good progress, the island of Jamaica disappearing entirely from view. Once night fell, the Spaniards took it in turns to keep watch or lookout and some of the Indians rested while the others paddled. The Spaniards were anxious lest the Indians, what with the heat and the shortage of drinking water, should do something that might endanger them all. By the next day they were all very weary but both captains egged their men on and they also took turns at the paddles insisting that everyone should eat to keep their strength up after such a long night's work. In this fashion they kept going though all they could see around them was the sea and the sky. . . .

The captains, who had charge of the small water casks, encouraged them by allowing them a sip or two every now and again and in this way kept them going until the cool of the evening was upon them. Apart from the raging thirst they suffered as a result of paddling non-stop for two days and a night, they were obsessed with the notion that they might have drifted off their intended course which was supposed to take them to the small island of Navasa, some eight leagues, as we say, from Hispaniola, for they hoped to be able to rest and recover there.

That same evening they had consigned to the waves the body of one of the Indians who had died from lack of water, and others had already fainted and were lying flat out on the floor or bottom of the canoes. Those who had proved stronger and fitter and were still upright were nevertheless very pessimistic and frightened that they, too, would drop dead at any moment as their colleague had done. Their last resort was to wet their mouths with salt water though, in the long run, that only exacerbated their discomfort. They drove themselves forward with what little strength they had left and when night fell for a second time and they had still not caught as much as a glimpse of the island, their despair was even greater.

God was pleased to lift their hearts and, as the moon came up, Diego Méndez noticed that half of it was obscured by the island, rather in the manner of an eclipse. They were all delighted and buoyed up by the prospect and, pointing to the island and giving the Indians some more water to drink, they set about paddling for it as fast as they could. Even then, it was dawn before they reached it and struggled ashore. They found the island to be half a league in circumference and covered in bare rock and they gave thanks to the Lord for having taken pity on them in their plight and rescued them from such peril. Their prime consideration was fresh water and the island was completely without trees and had no springs at all, consisting as it did of nothing but bare rock. But, by going from rock to rock, they found rain water aplenty lying in clefts and depressions in the rock—what are known as *xagüeyes* in the Indian tongue—and there was enough for them to fill their thirsty bellies and also the gourds they carried with them. Even then, their troubles were not over for they drank so fast because they were so parched and had gone without water for so long that some of the poor Indians dropped dead on the spot and others were violently sick. The upshot was that hardly any of them, if any at all, had the good fortune to see his native land again.

Those who were in a shape to do so spent the whole of that day resting and relaxing, cooked shellfish they found down by the water's edge, for Diego Méndez had brought the wherewithal to kindle a fire. They were now in sight of the end of this island [Hispaniola], christened by the admiral San Miguel and known to us today as Cape Tiburón, and were both eager to complete their journey and concerned that the weather might turn against them. So, come nightfall, they set out again, paddling for that headland and reaching it by daybreak on the fourth day after they originally set out. They spent two days there resting, after which Bartolomeo Fieschi announced his intention to comply with the admiral's orders and return to Jamaica. But both Indians and Spaniards were afraid of exposing themselves to more dangers of the kind they had just experienced and refused to go with him. He was therefore unable to return and I know nothing about what happened to him or to the Indians from that day onwards, and have no idea where they went.

Diego Méndez, who was in great haste to get on with the next part of his mission, followed the coast round as far as he could in his canoe. I do not know where he decided to leave it, but I believe that he availed himself of the presence of the Indians to carry his belongings and so I think it highly likely that none of them ever saw his wife and children again and that all of them spent the rest of their lives in wretched servitude. He finally reached the province and harbor of Xaraguá. . . .

When Diego Méndez reached Xaraguá he handed the admiral's letter to the commander-in-chief and explained to him where he had come from and how he had got there. The commander-in-chief appeared to be pleased at his arrival, even though he delayed his departure for a long while. . . . Finally, Diego Méndez's persistence won the day and he secured permission at least for himself to travel here to the city and harbor of Santo Domingo to set in train what the admiral, his master, had ordered. When he got here, he used the admiral's Hispaniola income to purchase a ship and load it with vital supplies and foodstuffs before sending it off to Jamaica towards the end of May fifteen hundred and four. He himself then set off for Spain, in accordance with the admiral's instructions.

3

The Spanish Crown, Portugal, and the Papacy

23

ALEXANDER VI

Papal Bull "Inter Cetera II"

Rome, May 4, 1493

This is the second of two bulls, both entitled "Inter Cetera," issued by Pope Alexander VI in an effort to settle the dispute between the Spanish and Portuguese crowns over their respective spheres in the Atlantic, which Columbus's first voyage had brought to a head. The official date of this bull is incorrect; it was actually issued in June 1493. This document, and Documents 24, 25, and 27, are written in the technical and highly stylized Renaissance Latin of the Papal Chancery.

Bishop Alexander, servant of the servants of God, to his dearest son in Christ, Fernando, and his dearest daughter in Christ, Isabel, illustrious king and queen of Castile, León, Aragón, Sicily, and Granada, greetings and apostolic blessing.

Among the other works pleasing to the divine majesty and dear to our heart, it is certainly foremost that the Catholic faith and Christian religion should especially be exalted in our times and be expanded and spread everywhere, and that the salvation of souls should be secured and barbarous nations should be subdued and led to the faith.

Geoffrey Symcox and Giovanna Rabitti, eds., Peter D. Diehl, trans., *Italian Reports on America 1493–1522: Letters, Dispatches, and Papal Bulls,* Repertorium Columbianum 10 (Turnhout, Belgium: Brepols, 2001), 34–37.

Therefore, since we have been called to this holy See of Peter by the favor of divine clemency despite our unworthiness, and recognizing you as true Catholic kings and rulers, such as we know you always have been, and which your deeds known to almost the entire world demonstrate famously, which you did not merely desire, but achieved with every effort, zeal, and diligence, sparing no labors, no expenses, and no dangers, even shedding your own blood, and dedicating your entire soul and all your toils now for a long time as the recovery of the kingdom of Granada from the tyranny of the Saracens, achieved by you just now with such great glory for the divine name testifies, we are properly and not undeservedly induced and are even obligated to grant to you willingly and favorably those things through which you can pursue this holy and praiseworthy enterprise, pleasing to immortal God, more fervently in days to come for the honor of God himself and the expansion of the Christian domain. We have learned that you had long ago proposed in spirit to seek out and discover other islands and mainlands, distant and unknown, and not found thus far by others, so that you might bring their natives and inhabitants to worship our Redeemer and profess the Catholic faith, but you were entirely occupied in the conquest and recovery of the same kingdom of Granada and could not bring your holy and laudable proposal to its desired goal.

But at last, as it has pleased the Lord, since the aforesaid kingdom has been recovered, wishing to fulfill your desire, you sent our beloved son Christopher Columbus, an especially worthy and entirely commendable man and well suited to such a great venture, with ships and men prepared for like enterprises, not without the greatest labors, expenses, and dangers, so that they might diligently seek out distant and unknown mainlands and islands of this sort in the sea where nobody had yet sailed. Sailing in the Ocean Sea with divine aid and with great diligence, they have now discovered certain very distant islands and also mainlands, which had not yet been found by others. In these very many peoples dwell who live peaceably and, it is asserted, go about naked and do not eat meat; and as far as your said envoys are able to suppose, the peoples dwelling in the said islands and lands believe that there is one creator god in the heavens, and they appear to be well prepared to embrace the Catholic faith and to be instructed in good morals; and it is hoped that if they were educated, the name of our Savior the Lord Jesus Christ would easily be brought into those lands and islands. And in one of the principal islands, the said Christopher caused to be built and erected a well fortified tower in which he placed certain Christians who had gone with him as a garrison, and so that they might search for other distant and unknown islands and mainlands. In the islands and lands already discovered, gold, spices, and very many other precious things of various sorts and quality are found; whence after having considered all these things and especially the exaltation and diffusion of the Catholic faith, as befits Catholic kings and rulers, in the manner of your ancestors, kings of illustrious memory, you have proposed to subject the said islands and mainlands and their natives and inhabitants to yourselves and to bring them to the Catholic faith, divine clemency willing.

Commending therefore your holy and laudable proposal highly in the Lord and desiring that it be brought to a proper conclusion and that the name of our Savior be brought into those regions, we urge you ardently in the Lord, and we require you strictly through the reception of holy baptism, by which you have been obligated to apostolic commands, and by the innermost mercy of our Lord Jesus Christ, that since you intend to pursue and take up an expedition of this sort willingly out of zeal for the orthodox faith, you should want to, and indeed you must, induce the peoples dwelling in these islands and mainlands to receive the Christian religion, nor should dangers or labors ever deter you at any time, since you have received the firm faith and confidence that almighty God will further your efforts propitiously. And so that you may more freely and more boldly take on the duty of so great an enterprise, given by the generosity of apostolic grace, by our own impulse, not at your instance nor that of another's petition offered to us on your behalf, but from our pure liberality and from certain knowledge and from the plenitude of apostolic power, we give, grant, and assign to you and your heirs and successors as kings of Castile and León, in perpetuity all islands and mainlands found or yet to be found, discovered and yet to be discovered towards the south and west. And by the authority granted to us by almighty God through St. Peter and the vicariate of Jesus Christ which we exercise on earth, we grant them with all their lordships, cities, castles, places and towns, rights and jurisdictions and all things appertaining thereto, by the tenor of the present letters, we give, grant, and assign to you and your heirs and successors, kings of Castile and León, and we make and establish a line from the Arctic pole (that is, the North) to the Antarctic pole (that is, the South), whether mainlands and islands are discovered and yet to be discovered towards India or towards any other region whatsoever. This line shall lie one hundred leagues to the south and west from any of the islands which are commonly called the Azores and Cape Verde, provided that all islands and mainlands found or yet to be found, discovered or yet to be discovered, from the said line to the west and south were not possessed in actuality by any Christian king or ruler, up to the day of Christmas last, from which the present year 1493 begins, when some of the said islands were discovered by your envoys and captains. And by the tenor of these present letters, we create, constitute, and depute you and your said heirs and successors as lords of them with full, free, and complete power, authority, and jurisdiction. We decree also through this our donation, grant, and assignment that the right thus acquired cannot be understood to be taken away from nor should be stripped from any Christian ruler who actually possessed the said islands and lands up to the said Christmas day.

And furthermore, we command you by virtue of holy obedience that, just as you have promised (and on account of your very great devotion and royal magnanimity we do not doubt that you will do it), you should send to the said mainlands and islands prudent and God-fearing men, learned, skilled, and proven, to instruct the said natives and inhabitants in the Catholic faith and to instill good morals in them, and that you should show all due diligence in these matters. And we strictly prohibit all persons whatsoever of whatever dignity, even royal or imperial, of whatever status, degree, order or condition, under penalty of excommunication *latae sententiae*,[1] which they shall incur immediately if they act against it, that they should not presume to travel to the islands and mainlands, discovered or yet to be discovered, found or yet to be found, towards the west and south, drawing and establishing a line from the Arctic pole to the Antarctic pole, whether mainlands and islands are found or are yet to be found towards India or towards any other region, which line shall lie one hundred leagues to the west from any of the islands which are commonly called the Azores and Cape Verde, as is said above, for the sake of acquiring wares or any other reason whatsoever without specific permission from you or your said heirs and successors, notwithstanding any contrary apostolic constitutions and ordinations and any other rights whatsoever. We trust in Him, from whom empires and lordships and all other good things proceed, that with the Lord guiding your actions, if you pursue this holy and laudable proposal, your labors and

---

[1]Excommunication *latae sententiae* was a form of excommunication which took effect as soon as a person committed specified offenses rather than only after an ecclesiastical court pronounced sentence.

efforts will achieve a most glorious result in a short time, bringing blessedness and glory for all the Christian people.

But because it would be difficult to send the present letter to every place whatsoever in which it might be expedient to do so, by like impulse and knowledge, we desire and decree that the same undoubted credence be given unreservedly in court and outside of court and everywhere else to copies of it which have been subscribed by the hand of a public notary employed for this purpose and ratified with the seal of some person established in ecclesiastical office or of an ecclesiastical court, as would be given to the present letter, if it were exhibited or shown.

Let no man therefore presume with rash boldness to violate or to contravene this page of our commendation, exhortation, requisition, donation, assignment, constitution, deputation, decree, mandate, prohibition, and will. If, however, anyone should dare to attempt this, let him know that he will incur the wrath of almighty God and of his apostles Peter and Paul. Given at Rome, at St. Peter's, in the year of Our Lord's incarnation 1493, the fourth of May, in the first year of our pontificate.

24

ALEXANDER VI

Papal Bull "Piis Fidelium"

Rome, June 25, 1493

Among the 1,200 to 1,300 men who departed for the Indies on Columbus's second voyage were the Franciscan monk Bernardo Buil and twelve other ecclesiastics, who were charged by Pope Alexander VI in this bull to begin converting the native population to Christianity. Buil brought with him the equipment necessary to establish the first church in the Indies, a gift of Queen Isabel.

Geoffrey Symcox and Giovanna Rabitti, eds., Peter D. Diehl, trans., *Italian Reports on America 1493–1522: Letters, Dispatches, and Papal Bulls,* Repertorium Columbianum 10 (Turnhout, Belgium: Brepols, 2001), 39–41.

Bishop Alexander, servant of the servants of God, to his beloved son Bernardo Buil, brother of the Friars Minor, vicar of the said order in the kingdoms of the Spains, greeting and apostolic blessing.

We gladly assent to the pious vows of the faithful, and especially those of Catholic kings and princes, which regard the propagation of religion and the augmentation of holy worship and the exaltation of the Catholic faith and the salvation of souls, and we further them with appropriate favors, as much as we can with God. Since, just as our dearest son in Christ Fernando and our dearest daughter in Christ Isabel, the illustrious king and queen of Castile and León, Aragón and Granada, have recently caused to be explained to us, they were inflamed with the fervor of devotion and wanted the Catholic faith to flourish and be exalted in the lands and islands newly discovered by them towards the western regions and the Ocean Sea, some previously unknown and some yet to be discovered, and so they determined to send you to those regions, so that you might preach and sow the word of God there by yourself and through other secular or religious priests suited to the purpose and to be deputed by you, and that you should lead the natives and inhabitants of the said islands and lands, who do not have a knowledge of our faith, to that faith and the Christian religion, and that you should teach and instruct them to walk in the mandates of the Lord. Hoping that you will perform faithfully and diligently those things which we have caused to be assigned to you, we grant and bestow upon you, who are a priest, in the tenor of the present letter, by apostolic authority and from certain knowledge, full, free, and comprehensive ability, permission, power, and authority: (1) to go to the said islands and regions with various associates of your order or another chosen by you or the same king and queen, with no permission of your superiors or of any other whatsoever required, and to remain there as long as you want, (2) and to preach and sow the word of God by yourself or by another or several other secular or religious priests of whatever order suitable for the task, bringing the said natives and inhabitants to the Catholic faith, and baptizing them and instructing them in the faith, (3) and to administer the sacraments of the church to them as often as necessary, and to hear them and any one of them in their confessions by yourself or by any secular or religious priest as often as necessary, and to provide concerning the debt of absolution, and to assign them a salutary penance when the crimes, excesses, and sins committed by them have been diligently heard, even if they should be such that on account of them the Apostolic See should be consulted in any way whatsoever, and also to commute whatever vows sworn by them into other works of piety, excepting vows of religion or of pilgrimage to Jerusalem, the tombs of the apostles Peter and Paul, and of St. James in Compostela, (4) and to erect, construct, and build whatever churches, chapels, monasteries, houses of any and all orders, even of mendicants, both for men and for women, and holy places, with bell-towers, bells, cloisters, dormitories, refectories, gardens, garden sheds, and all other necessary work-shops, and to receive houses for the professors of the mendicant orders, which you shall have constructed and built for them, and to grant them perpetual license to dwell there, and to bless the said churches, and however often it may happen that they and their ceme-teries are violated by the shedding of blood or semen or otherwise, to reconcile them with water blessed beforehand by any Catholic priest, as is customary, (5) and also in time of necessity, concerning which we lay the burden on your conscience, to freely and licitly partake of meats and other foods forbidden to you and your said associates according to the regular institutions of the said orders, and to do, exercise, carry out, and arrange each and every thing necessary and opportune for these affairs in any way whatsoever. For this we grant the ability, license, power, and authority by the tenor of these present letters.

And furthermore, so that Christians may more willingly flock to those islands and lands for the sake of devotion, by which they may hope to gain the salvation of their souls, we grant to each and every of the aforesaid Christians of both sexes who will personally bring them-selves to the said lands and islands, but with the permission and man-date of the said king and queen, that each and every one of them may choose a suitable secular or religious confessor who may absolve them and theirs in the aforesaid way from their crimes, sins, and transgres-sions, even those reserved to the said Apostolic See, and may com-mute their vows, and may be able to grant indulgence and remission of all their sins of which they have confessed with contrite heart and mouth, to those who remain in the sincerity of the faith, in the unity of the holy Roman Church, and in obedience and devotion to us and to our successors entering canonically as Roman pontiffs, once in life and once in the embrace of death, by the aforesaid authority.

We also grant, as a gift of special grace and by the said authority, to monasteries, places, and houses which are to be erected and built, and to the monks and friars dwelling in them at the time, that they may freely and licitly use, acquire, and enjoy each and every grace, privilege, liberty, exemption, immunity, indulgence, and grant conceded or yet to be conceded in general to other monasteries, places, houses, monks, and brothers of the orders to which they belong, notwithstanding the constitutions of our predecessor, pope Boniface VIII of blessed memory, that no brothers whatsoever of the mendicant orders should presume to receive new places without a special license of the Apostolic See which makes full and express mention of this prohibition, and notwithstanding other apostolic constitutions and also the statutes and customs of the said orders ratified by oath, apostolic confirmation, or any other authorization, and notwithstanding that you are not among the persons established in ecclesiastical dignity, to whom apostolic letters should be directed, and notwithstanding all other contrary constitutions.

But because it would be difficult to send the present letter to every place whatsoever in which it might be expedient to do so, by the said authority, we desire and decree that the same undoubted credence be given unreservedly in court and outside court and everywhere else to copies of it which have been subscribed by the hand of a public notary employed for this purpose and ratified with the seal of some person established in ecclesiastical office, or of an ecclesiastical court, as would be given to the present letter if it were exhibited or shown.

Let no man therefore presume with rash boldness to violate or to contravene this page of our concession, grant, will, indulgence, and decree. If anyone should dare to attempt this, let him know that he will incur the wrath of almighty God and of his apostles Peter and Paul. Given in Rome, at St. Peter's, in the year of Our Lord's incarnation 1493, the twenty-fifth of June, in the first year of our pontificate.

25

ALEXANDER VI

Papal Bull "Dudum Siquidem"

Rome, September 25, 1493

---

*This bull amplified and extended the grant of sovereignty over the lands
claimed by the Spanish crown in the West Indies, originally set out in
"Inter Cetera II."*

Bishop Alexander, servant of the servants of God, to his dearest son
in Christ, Fernando, and his dearest daughter in Christ, Isabel, king
and queen of Castile, León, Aragón, and Granada, greetings and apostolic blessing.

Recently we gave, granted, and assigned to you and your heirs and
successors as kings of Castile and León in perpetuity all the islands
and mainlands found or yet to be found towards the west and south,
which were not at present under the temporal domination of any
Christian lords, by our own impulse and from certain knowledge and
from the fullness of apostolic power, investing you and your said successors with them; and we established and deputed you as lords of
them with full, free, and manifold power, authority, and jurisdiction,
just as is more fully contained in our letters composed for that purpose, the tenor of which we wish to be considered to be fully expressed here, as if it were inserted word for word in the present letter.
Since, moreover, it could happen that your envoys and captains or vas-
sals sailing toward the west and south might steer to eastern regions
and find islands and mainlands which had been or were discovered,
therefore wishing also to honor you with gracious favors, by like
impulse, knowledge, and plenitude of apostolic power, we likewise
extend and expand the said gift, grant, assignment, and letters, with
each and every clause contained in the same letters, to each and
every island and mainland found or yet to be found, discovered or yet
to be discovered, which have been or will be discovered or will appear

Geoffrey Symcox and Giovanna Rabitti, eds., Peter D. Diehl, trans., *Italian Reports on
America 1493–1522: Letters, Dispatches, and Papal Bulls,* Repertorium Columbianum 10
(Turnhout, Belgium: Brepols, 2001), 41–43.

by sailing or traveling to the west or south in such a way, whether they are in regions of the West or the South or the East or of India, by apostolic authority entirely in the tenor of the present letter in all things and for all things, as if a full and express mention had been made of them in the said letters.

We grant to you and your said heirs and successors full and free permission to take physical possession of the said islands and lands freely by your own authority in person or through another or others, and to keep them perpetually, and also to defend them against all who oppose you, and we strictly forbid all persons whatsoever of any dignity, status, degree, order, or condition whatsoever under penalty of excommunication *latae sententiae,* which they will incur immediately by acting against it, that they should not presume without express and specific permission from you or your said heirs and successors, under any pretext or color, to go or send to the said regions for sailing, fishing, or exploring islands or mainlands, notwithstanding any apostolic constitutions or ordinations or any donations, grants, permissions, and assignments whatsoever made by us or our predecessors to anybody, whether kings or princes, *infantes,* or any other persons, or to religious orders or military orders concerning the said regions, seas, islands, and lands, or any part of them, from all causes whatsoever, even if it be out of piety or the faith, or for the redemption of captives, and other most urgent causes, however great; and with any provisions whatsoever, even those derogatory to those who derogate them, stronger, more effective and uncustomary, and containing in them any sentences, censures, and penalties whatsoever save those excluded by real and present possession, even if those to whom donations and grants of this sort had been made, or their envoys, may have sailed there at some time. We consider the import of those as sufficiently expressed in the present letter, and with like impulse, knowledge, and plenitude of power, we revoke them entirely, and concerning the islands and lands not at present occupied, we want them to be considered null and void, and also all those things which we desired not to obstruct them in the said letters, and all other contrary provisions whatsoever.

Given at Rome, at St. Peter's, in the year of the Lord's incarnation fourteen hundred ninety three, on the twenty-fifth of September, in the second year of our pontificate.

26

Treaty of Tordesillas between Spain and Portugal

June 7, 1494

The Treaty of Tordesillas, signed June 7, 1494, was intended to resolve a long-standing dispute between the kingdoms of Spain and Portugal, a dispute that became crucial after Columbus's first voyage of discovery to the Indies. The treaty established a line of demarcation in the Atlantic Ocean—running from the North Pole to the South Pole on a longitude 370 leagues west of the Cape Verde Islands—and authorized Spanish exploration of the lands to the west of the line and Portuguese exploration and colonization of the lands to the east.

Be it manifest and known to all who shall see this public instrument that at the village of Tordesillas on the seventh day of the month of June in the year of the nativity of our Lord Jesus Christ 1494 in the presence of us, the secretaries, clerks, and notaries public subscribed below, there being present the honorable Sir Enrique Enriques, chief steward of the very exalted and very mighty princes the lord and lady Sir Fernando and Lady Isabel, by the grace of God king and queen of Castile, León, Aragón, Sicily, Granada, etc., Sir Gutierrez de Cardenas, chief auditor of the said lords, the king and queen, and Doctor Rodrigo Maldonado, all members of the council of the said lords, the king and queen of Castile, León, Aragón, Sicily, Granada, etc., their qualified representatives of the one part, and the honorable Ruy de Sousa, lord of Sagres and Berenguel, Sir Juan de Sousa, his son, chief inspector of weights and measures of the very exalted and very excellent lord João, by the grace of God king of Portugal and of the Algarves on this side and beyond the sea in Africa, lord of Guinea, and Ayres de Almada, magistrate of civil cases in his court, all of the council of the said lord king of Portugal, and his qualified ambassadors and representatives, as was proved by both the parties by means of the letters of authorization and procurations from the said lords their constituents ...

Frances Gardiner Davenport, ed., *European Treaties Bearing on the History of the United States and Its Dependencies,* 4 vols. (Washington DC: Carnegie Institution of Washington 1917–1939) 1.93–100.

It was declared by the above-mentioned representatives of the aforesaid king and queen of Castile, León, Aragón, Sicily, Granada, etc., and of the aforesaid king of Portugal and the Algarves, etc.:

That, whereas a certain controversy exists between the said lords, their constituents, as to what lands, of all those discovered in the ocean sea up to the present days, the date of this treaty, pertain to each one of the said parts respectively; therefore, for the sake of peace and concord, and for the preservation of the relationship and love of the king of Portugal for the king and queen of Castile, Aragón, etc., it being the pleasure of their highnesses, they, their representatives, acting in their name and by virtue of their powers herein described, covenanted and agreed that a boundary or straight line be determined and drawn north and south, from pole to pole, on the ocean sea, from the Arctic to the Antarctic pole. This boundary or line shall be drawn straight, as aforesaid, at a distance of three hundred and seventy leagues west of the Cape Verde Islands, being calculated by degrees, or by any other manner as may be considered the best and readiest, provided the distance shall be no greater than abovesaid. And all lands, both islands and mainlands, found and discovered already, or to be found and discovered hereafter, by the king of Portugal and by his vessels on this side of the line and boundary determined as above, toward the east, in either north or south latitude, on the eastern side of the boundary, provided the boundary is not crossed, shall belong to, and remain in the possession of, and pertain forever to the king of Portugal and his successors. And all other lands, both islands and mainlands, found or to be found hereafter, discovered or to be discovered hereafter, which have been discovered or shall be discovered by the king and queen of Castile, Aragón, etc., and by their vessels, on the western side of the boundary, determined as above, after having passed the boundary toward the west, in either its north or south latitude, shall belong to, and remain in the possession of and pertain forever to the king and queen of Castile, León, etc., and to their successors.

Item, the said representatives promise and affirm by virtue of the powers aforesaid that from this date no ships shall be dispatched— namely, as follows: the king and queen of Castile, León, Aragón, etc., for this part of the boundary and its eastern side on this side of the boundary, which pertains to the king of Portugal and the Algarves, etc.; nor the king of Portugal to the other part of the said boundary which pertains to the king and queen of Castile, León, Aragón, etc.— for the purpose of discovering and seeking any mainlands or islands, or for the purpose of trade, barter, or conquest of any kind. But should it come to pass that the ships of the king and queen of Castile, León, Aragón, etc., sailing on this side of the boundary, should discover any mainlands or islands in the region pertaining to the king of Portugal, such mainlands or islands shall pertain to and belong forever to the king of Portugal and his heirs, and their highnesses shall order them to be surrendered to him immediately. And if the ships of the king of Portugal discover any islands and mainlands in the regions of the king and queen of Castile, León, Aragón, etc., all such lands shall belong to and remain forever in the possession of the king and queen of Castile, León, Aragón, etc., and their heirs, and the king of Portugal shall cause such lands to be surrendered immediately.

. . .

Item, inasmuch as the ships of the king and queen of Castile, León, and Aragón, etc., sailing as before declared, from their kingdoms to their possessions on the other side of the said line, must cross the seas on this side of the line, pertaining to the king of Portugal, it is therefore concerted and agreed that the ships of the king and queen of Castile, León, Aragón, etc., shall, at any time and without any hindrance, sail in either direction, freely, securely, and peacefully, over the seas of the king of Portugal, and within the line. And whenever their highnesses and their successors wish to do so, and deem it expedient, their ships may take their courses and routes direct from their kingdoms to any region within their line and boundary to which they desire to dispatch expeditions of discovery, conquest, and trade. They shall take their courses direct to the desired region and for any purpose desired therein, and shall not leave their course unless compelled to do so by contrary weather. They shall do this provided that, before crossing the said line, they shall not seize or take possession of anything discovered in this region by the king of Portugal; and should their ships find anything before crossing the line, as aforesaid, it shall belong to the king of Portugal, and their highnesses shall order it surrendered immediately. . . .

27

ALEXANDER VI

Papal Bull "Eximie Devotionis"

Rome, November 16, 1501

This bull constitutes another step in the process of establishing the Catholic Church in the Spanish colonies in the Americas, begun by "Piis Fidelium" in 1493. It authorizes the levying of tithes to support the clergy and to pay for the building of churches there.

Bishop Alexander, servant of the servants of God, to his dearest son in Christ, Fernando, and his dearest daughter in Christ, Isabel, Catholic king and queen of the Spains, greeting and apostolic blessing.

The sincerity of extraordinary devotion and the complete faith by which you revere us and the Roman Church not unworthily merit that you be able to attend more promptly and more willingly to your vows, and especially to those concerning the exaltation of the Catholic faith and the subjugation of barbarous and infidel nations. Indeed a petition on your behalf just now shown to us stated that you, induced by pious devotion, wish most of all for the exaltation of the Catholic faith, just as you already began to do from a certain time onward, not without great expense and great toils on your part, and to the present day you continue to do ever more to recover and acquire islands and regions of the Indies, so that in those places, after every damned sect has been cast down, the Highest may be worshiped and venerated. And since for the recovery of the said islands and regions it will be necessary for you to sustain serious expenses and endure great dangers, it is expedient for the preservation and retention of the said islands, after they have been acquired and recovered by you, that you may be able to exact and raise tithes of the said islands from their natives and inhabitants living there at the time for those necessary expenses which must be sustained for the said retention and preservation. Therefore it was humbly beseeched of us on your behalf, that we

---

Geoffrey Symcox and Giovanna Rabitti, eds., Peter D. Diehl, trans., *Italian Reports on America 1493–1522: Letters, Dispatches, and Papal Bulls,* Repertorium Columbianum 10 (Turnhout, Belgium: Brepols, 2001), 58–59.

should deign from apostolic benevolence to provide suitably for you and your state in the aforesaid matters.

We therefore, who desire with our highest affections the exaltation and expansion of that same faith especially in our late times, and who most highly commend your proposal in the Lord, and who favor supplications of this sort, by a gift of special grace grant to you and your successors in times to come, by apostolic authority in the tenor of the present letter, that you may freely and licitly receive and levy the tithe in this way in the said islands from their natives and inhabitants, after they have been acquired and recovered, as is stated, once a sufficient endowment has first been assigned really and effectively to the churches which will be erected in the said islands by you and your said successors, according to the ordination of the diocesan bishops of the places then serving, whose consciences we charge in this matter, from your goods and theirs, from which endowment those governing them and their rectors may be able to maintain themselves appropriately and to carry out the duties incumbent on the said churches at the time and to perform divine worship and the praise of almighty God properly, and to pay episcopal dues, notwithstanding the constitutions of the Lateran Council[1] and others, and the apostolic statutes and all other contrary measures whatsoever.

Let no man therefore presume with rash boldness to violate or to contravene this page of our concession. If, however, anyone should dare to attempt this, let him know that he will incur the wrath of almighty God and of his apostles Peter and Paul.

Given at Rome, at St. Peter's in the year of the Lord's incarnation one thousand five hundred one, the sixteenth of November, in the tenth year of our pontificate.

---

[1]Presumably a reference to canons 52, 53, and 54 of the Fourth Lateran Council (1215).

4

European Constructions of the New World

28

ALLEGRETTO ALLEGRETTI

Sienese Diaries from 1450 to 1496

April 25, 1493

Allegretto Allegretti was born in Siena in 1429 to a family of bankers and money changers. He served as commissioner general of the Republic of Siena and died in 1497. The information he reports is taken from Columbus's "Letter to Santángel," published a month or so earlier.

The king of Spain discovered many islands again this year, that is, in the Canaries, beyond the Pillars of Hercules; there his captain Christopher Columbus, captain of the galleys, discovered various sorts of men with divers customs; he discovered islands with gold and many kinds of spices, and some islands where the men do no work, but live on what the land produces. On one island there are men who eat other men from a nearby island, and they are great enemies to each other and do not have any type of weapons. Their seas are very tranquil, and they ply them using certain large tree trunks dug out forcefully with certain sharp stones. We know this by way of several letters from our merchants in Spain, and by word of mouth from several people. We have also learned that the captain of the fleet left about eighty men to guard an island, and they fortified a position for themselves as best they could. The people were happy to see the king of

Geoffrey Symcox and Luciano Formisano, eds., Theodore J. Cachey Jr. and John C. McLucas, trans., *Italian Reports on America 1493–1522: Accounts by Contemporary Observers,* Repertorium Columbianum 12 (Turnhout, Belgium: Brepols, 2002), 27.

Spain's men and welcomed them with great honor, kindnesses, presents, and gifts; among these they presented the Spaniards with many young virgins. After observing our customs, clothing, and the practice of our trades, they hold our men to be gods; for this reason the king of Spain wants to send many caravels loaded with supplies for all the trades in order to instruct and train those men. The Spaniards brought back to Spain about thirty of them to learn the language and customs, intending to take them back to the islands as interpreters.

29

MORELLETTO PONZONE

Letter from Ferrara

June 11, 1494

Morelletto Ponzone came from a prominent family of Cremona. In this letter to Isabella, the daughter of Ercole I d'Este, duke of Ferrara, and wife of Francesco II Gonzaga, reporting news of Columbus's second voyage, he describes the captive Indians presented at court by Columbus. They were intended to serve not only as exotic trophies; they were to be converted to Christianity and taught the Castilian language so that they could serve as interpreters and intermediaries between the Spanish colonists and their own people in the Indies.

To my illustrious lady, the marchioness of Mantua in Mantua.

As for news of Spain, recently someone called Columbus has found a certain island for the king of Spain, in which there are men of our stature, but they are brown-skinned and they have noses like apes and the leader of them has a piece of gold stuck in his nose which covers his mouth and is four fingers wide; and the women have a broad face like a disk, and they all go naked, men and women. And he brought twelve of them and four women to the king of Spain, and they are so weak by nature that two fell ill in Seville in such a way that the physi-

---

Geoffrey Symcox and Giovanna Rabitti, eds., Peter D. Diehl, trans., *Italian Reports on America 1493–1522: Letters, Dispatches, and Papal Bulls,* Repertorium Columbianum 10 (Turnhout, Belgium: Brepols, 2001), 45.

cians did not understand their illness, and they did not find a pulse, and they were dead; the others have been dressed, and when they see a well dressed person, they run their hands along his back and they kiss their own hands, which pleases them. Then they instructed them and they have understanding, and they are lethargic, and nobody understands their language; but they eat at the table and they eat everything, and they do not give them wine; in their country, they eat the roots of grasses and a certain thing which resembles pepper, big as a nut, which yields great substance, and thus do they live. And under their rocks, by lifting them up one finds plenty of gold, which is beautiful, and it only needs to be refined; for the other matters I will give notice of what will follow. Dated Ferrara, 11 June 1494, your servant, Morelletto Ponzone of Cremona.

30

DIEGO ALVAREZ CHANCA

From His *Report to the City Council of Seville on Columbus's Second Voyage*

ca. 1494

Diego Alvarez Chanca (ca. 1463–ca. 1515) accompanied Columbus on his second voyage to the Indies. In 1492 he held the position of physician to Fernando and Isabel, and in 1493 the Spanish monarchs requested that Chanca accompany Columbus on his second voyage to the Indies as physician to the fleet. His report on the voyage, which took the form of a letter to the city council of his native city Seville, reveals his reaction to the natural sights of the New World and his amazement at the diversity of flora and fauna.

On this island [Mariagalante] the density of wooded areas was a marvel, and the variety of types of trees was astonishing—some with flowers, others with fruit—so that there was greenery everywhere. We found there a tree whose foliage gave off the purest smell of

Luciano Gallinari, ed., *Diego Alvarez Chanca, Medico di Cristoforo Colombo* (Cagliari, Italy: Istituto sui Rapporti Italo-Iberici, 1992), 243–44, 266–68.

cloves that I have ever encountered, and it resembled a laurel except it was not as large. There was an unusual different type of wild fruit [the machineel, or "poison apple"], which some of the less cautious men sampled; just touching the fruit with their tongues caused their faces to swell and resulted in such intense heat and pain that they seemed to be in agony and had to be treated with cold things. On this island we found no people and no signs of them; we believed it to be uninhabited, and were there about two hours, for when we arrived it was some time in the afternoon.

The next morning we left for another very big island [Guadeloupe] that seemed to lie behind this one at a distance of seven or eight leagues. We reached this island at a point near a large mountain that seemed to reach the sky, in the middle of which was a peak taller than the rest of the mountain from which a great quantity of water fell in different streams, most intensely in our direction. Three leagues away a dense flood of water was visible, falling such a distance that it seemed to come from the heavens. It appeared to be so far away that the sailors began to place many wagers among themselves, some claiming that it was composed of feathers of birds, others that it was water. As we got closer we knew for sure, and it was the most beautiful thing in the world to see the distance which such a large quantity of water was falling and the very small place from which it originated.

· · ·

Although we have spent little time in observation, we have seen marvelous things, such as trees that bear fine wool, which those who know something of the art say could be woven into excellent cloth. There are so many of these trees that we could fill the ships with wool, although the wool is laborious to gather because the trees have spines and thus it takes a bit of ingenuity. There are a great number of evergreen trees as large as peach trees, and trees that bear a wax that is as fine as beeswax in color and taste and burns as well, so that there is no difference between the two. There are many fine and unusual turpentine trees, and also a great amount of very fine tragacanth. There are trees that I think are nutmeg, except that here they are fruitless; I think they are nutmeg because the taste and odor of the bark is like nutmeg. I saw a ginger root that an Indian was carrying hung around his neck; also there is aloe,[1] and although it is not of the type that is seen in our country there is no doubt that it is one of the

---

[1]The juice of aloe leaves was used as a purgative or a tonic.

types of aloe that doctors use. There is also a type of cinnamon, which admittedly is not as fine as that in Spain; we don't know if this is because by chance it was not gathered at the right time or if it is just an inferior type.

There are also yellow mirabelles, which here are always under the trees; as the earth is very humid they are rotten and have a very bitter taste, which I think can be attributed to the fact that they are spoiled, for in every other respect save for taste they are certainly mirabelles. There is also very fine mastic.

The people of these islands have never seen nor do they possess any iron; they have many tools, such as hatchets and adzes made of stone, which are so attractive and well-wrought that it is a marvel what can be done without iron.

Their food is bread made from the roots of a grass that is something in between a tree and grass [cassava or manioc], and sweet potatoes, which as I have already said is an excellent food. To season it they have a spice called *axí* [capsicum or chili] with which they also eat fish or birds when they can have them, of which there are many varieties. Furthermore they have grains like hazelnuts which are very good to eat. They eat snakes and lizards and spiders and many worms which are found in the soil; it seems to me that their selection of meat is as good as any in the world.

31

RAMÓN PANÉ

On Taino Religious Practices

ca. 1498

Friar Ramón Pané went to Hispaniola on Columbus's second voyage and at the admiral's request, starting early in 1495 and continuing for a period of several years, lived among the Indians of Hispaniola, learned their language, and observed and recorded their practices and beliefs. Pané's original report, which he submitted to Columbus around 1498,

Geoffrey Symcox and Luciano Formisano, eds., Theodore J. Cachey Jr. and John C. McLucas, trans., *Italian Reports on America 1493–1522: Accounts by Contemporary Observers,* Repertorium Columbianum 12 (Turnhout, Belgium: Brepols, 2002), 63–68.

has not survived, but a copy of it found its way to Ferrara, where the
merchant Giovanni de' Strozzi saw it and forwarded it to the Venetian
Alessandro Zorzi. Pané's short treatise is the first account of Indian cul-
ture based on ethnographic observation.

When in 1492 Christopher Columbus discovered the island of Hispaniola, among the other things reported was that the peoples of that
island did not worship anything other than the heavens, planets, and
stars. But after living there and learning the language, they became
familiar with those people and observed that they had various ceremonies and customs, as did the hermit friar Ramón [Pané], whom
Bartolomé Colón, brother of Christopher, brought from Rome to
that island in order to instruct and convert the islanders to our Christian faith. He composed a book about their customs, many of which
will be related in this letter. First, they say that there appear at night
on that island certain phantasms and visions of which they sense-
lessly make certain simulacra which they gather together to worship;
seated on the ground on blankets of cotton-wool they carve certain
good demons, just as among us there are sculptors. The simulacra
are called zemis [see Figure 6], and they worship them as eternal
gods; they say there are two, that is, one called Iocauna, and the other
elder one, Guamaonocon. These are said to have five mothers, named
Attabeira, Mamona, Guacarapita, Liella, and Guimazoa. There is a
region of that island which is called Caunana, where they say human-
kind first issued from grottos in two mountains, that is, the greater
part from the larger cave, and the lesser part from the smaller
cave. Those mountains are called Cauta; the larger cave is called
Cazibasagua, and the smaller one Amaiauna. The first to issue from
that cavern was called Machochael, who guarded the opening every
night. He once went out a short distance and saw the sun at dawn,
and since he was unable to endure that light, was transformed into a
stone. In the same way many others who went out at night from that
cavern to go fishing and who were unable to return before the sun
rose, upon seeing the light, as punishment since they were not permitted to see it, were immediately transformed into those trees which
yield plums. These grow spontaneously on that island in great quantity, without being planted. They also tell of a ruler named Vaguoniona, who sent his servant out of that cavern to go fishing; that
servant, since he was unable to return before the sun rose, was trans-

Figure 6. *A Zemi, a Taino Deity Figure*

Dominican Republic (?), Ironwood and shell, 68.4 cm.

Source: The Metropolitan Museum of Art, The Michael C. Rockefeller Memorial Collection, Bequest of Nelson A. Rockefeller (1979, 1979. 206.380).

formed into a nightingale.[1] Ever since then, during the night and in the same season in which he was transformed into a bird, he sings and laments his bad fortune and asks for help from his master Vaguoniona. It is for this reason that they say the nightingale sings at night. Afterwards Vaguoniona, who greatly loved his servant, left the cave,

---

[1] The nightingale is not indigenous to the Americas; this is probably a reference to the mocking bird.

bringing forth only the females with their nursing children; they went to an island not far from there which is called Matininó; there he left the females and brought back with him the little children. Afterwards, having been abandoned near a little river, they began to cry, uttering "toa, toa," that is, "mamma, mamma," so that they were changed into frogs. This is the reason they say that in the spring those frogs begin to sing. They say that men came out of those caverns in this way and spread throughout Hispaniola, without their women. They also say that Vaguoniona wandered about among different places and, by special grace, was never transformed, except by a beautiful female whom he saw in the sea. He descended into the sea and received from her certain marble pebbles which they call *cibas,* as well as certain little golden tablets which are called *guaninos.* These gems, to this day associated with their kings, are held in reverence as sacred things. The men who had remained in the cave without their females came out during the night, after washing themselves in ditches where a large amount of rainwater had gathered (and still today they use those baths). As soon as they had come out, it is said, they raced to the plum trees, upon which an infinite number of ants had gathered; they grasped them with their hands, as if they were so many females, and when they squeezed them they slipped out of their hands like eels. They went to seek counsel from elderly counselors, and they went to see if there were any men who might have scabies or leprosy or who might have calloused, rough hands with which they could easily hold the ants. Those men are called *caracaracoles;* thus they went to hunt them, and although they captured many, they were nevertheless unable to keep more than four, which they used as females. They say that they had no genitals, and for this reason it is said they returned to the elders for counsel; consequently they sent them the woodpecker, who, with his sharp beak, opened the genitals between the thighs of those females, and the others descended from there. Here it is certainly amazing that one reads that the Myrmidons, who are described by the Greeks in so many books, were descended from ants. Thus, in this way, their wise men, with gravity and reputation, from bowers and eminent places, instruct those simple islanders and persuade them to believe such things as these to be sacred and true. Concerning the origins of the sea, they say there was a very powerful man named Iaia on that island, who killed his only son, whom he placed in a gourd instead of in a fabricated tomb. Later, this Iaia, after having passed many months troubled by the death of his son, returned to that gourd and opened it, and a great whale issued forth. . . . Drawn by the report of this, four youths, born of a single birth, in the hopes of obtaining the fish within the gourd, took it in their hands. Iaia, who had enclosed the bones in the gourd, came upon them; the youths, frightened at their sacrilege, and to avoid being accused of that robbery by Iaia, tried to flee. The gourd, because of its great weight, fell upon the ground and broke, and the sea escaped through the cracks. The sea flowed down the valleys and across the great plains nearly filling them, except for the peaks of mountains and high places that were left uncovered, which created the islands which can presently be seen. They also say that those brothers, for fear of Iaia, fled to different places and were dying of hunger, for they did not have the courage to stop. They went to knock at the door of a baker, asking for cassava, that is, bread. Entering the house, they spat at the baker a deadly spit that killed him. Those brothers, after a discussion, opened him up with a sharp stone, and out of that wound a female was born, and those brothers slept with her together, and both males and females were the result. In addition to these things, they say there is a cave which is called Iovanaboina—named for a king of that country who is called Macchinnech—which is for them a more religious place than Santiago de Compostela is for us. It is adorned with many different paintings and has two doors sculpted to represent their demons, the zemis, one of which they call Bintaitalle, the other Marochum. When we asked them why they worship that cave with such devotion, they said that the sun and moon issued forth from there to illuminate the world. These senseless men affirm these things with great gravity, and there is as great an affluence of people coming and going from that cave as there is in our churches and at the great pilgrimage places. Another kind of superstition: they say that after death they wander about like vagabonds and that they live on the fruit of a tree which grows there, unknown to us, similar to our quince. They converse with the living, and take the form of men; they sleep with women and deceive them, and when they are about to consummate the act they become invisible. If by chance a woman, sensing something strange, suspects that she is in bed with a dead person (for some are known to murmur), she can tell the living from the dead by looking at the navel, since it is said that the dead can assume any human form except for the navel. They also believe that often at night they encounter dead people on the public roads, and if he who is walking is not afraid, it is said the phantasm will disappear, while if he is afraid, they continue in such a way that the people will be left injured and stupefied. When they were asked by our men where they learn those vain customs (which are a pestilence among them), they answer that they have been handed down from their ancestors; and that it is not permitted to teach such things and songs except to the sons of the kings; and that they never had writing among them and everything is preserved by memory. On festival days the people sing and make music, as we do on our holy days. They have only a single instrument, which is made of a concave piece of wood called *reboans,* which is like a drum. They have their priest-soothsayers, called *bohuti,* who imbue them with such superstition. There are also the doctors who teach a thousand senseless old plebeian women a thousand deceits. Likewise those soothsayers compel the plebeians to believe it all, because they have great authority over them, for they claim to speak with the zemis and to know all. The *bohuti* compel the people to fast and to purge themselves: they take a certain powder made from an herb, which they drink, and immediately they are seized by a frenzy and moan like drunken men. To effect cures, they take some stone pebbles or a piece of meat in their mouths. The *bohuti* circle around them three or four times, distorting their faces and their lips and making ugly gestures; they blow on the necks, the temples, and the foreheads of the sick; they grasp at the air, and say that they are taking away all the evil that they have in their veins and that makes them sick; they rub the thighs, legs, and pubis of the sick people, and with their hands held together they run toward the open door, and cast it out with their hands. They persuade them in this way that they have driven out the disease. The last of them holds in his mouth a piece of meat, just like a magician, and cries out saying that it was something he had eaten: "Now you will be well because I have removed the evil." And if he sees that the sick man does not get better, he leads the man to believe that his zemi is angry with him for not having honored the zemi as he should have, and for not having built for him some shrine. If the sick man should die, his relatives are compelled to confess that he died in spite of the efforts of the *bohuti,* for not having properly fasted, and for their not having given good medicines. If the *bohuti* doctors were the cause of his death, they take revenge upon that *bohuti.* Concerning those stones, or rather bones, which the *bohuti* held in his mouth, if those stones and bones are tied together and wrapped in cloth and preserved faithfully, they benefit greatly their children. Their females keep those stones and bones as they do zemis. The islanders believe in various zemis which they worship: those which come at night in visions and are seen among the trees, they carve in wood; others which answer them from among the rocks are carved in marble; others are found among the roots of the plants that they eat instead of bread, called sweet potatoes; those zemis are patrons of that bread because it is their food. Just as among the ancients the Dryads, Hamadryads, Satyrs, Pan, and the Nereids were patrons of the fountains, seas, and woods, so those islanders have each of them their zemis, whom they call upon when they are in need. Likewise, in the event of war, famine, or abundance . . . when their kings need counsel, they ask the zemis and go to the house dedicated to them. They sniff through their nostrils some of the powder called *cohoba,*[2] with the effect that the *bohuti* immediately are seized by a frenzy and have the impression that the entire house is reversing on its foundations and that the men are walking around upside down. *Cohoba* is so powerful that it immediately renders senseless persons who take it, so that they go crazy and their arms and legs go to sleep, and when their heads are cleared of the fumes a heavy sleepiness comes upon them; they twist their eyes to heaven and speak confusedly. The principal men of the house, who are alone (for they do not want any of the common people to witness the sacrifice), cry out in a loud voice for grace, at which point the *bohuti* say that the zemis have spoken with them. Then they relate what they saw, affirming that, when that inebriated one opened his mouth, it was the zemis who were speaking to him, telling him whether there would be famine or pestilence, an impending victory, or abundance. Whatever the future will bring, his zemis tell him all, just as the ancients say about the Apollonian spirit that inspired the Sibyls; it appears that the superstitions that were current among them have not disappeared, as one can see from what was said above about the zemis. Concerning particular deities there, we mention a few of those the islanders spoke about. They say a king called Guamareto had a zemi named Corochoto whom the king kept bound securely above the highest point of the house. That zemi, in order to copulate or perhaps to eat, would break his bonds and go hide himself in certain mountain cliffs, and he would remain in hiding for a few days, vexed because the king Guamareto had been deficient in his prayers on the holy days. They also say that in that region in a town of Guamareto a boy born with two crowns was believed to be the son of the zemi Corochoto. They say that king Guamareto was defeated in battle by his enemy, and his house was destroyed and his city burned and put to the sword; it is said that Corochoto escaped from his bonds

---

[2]A hallucinogenic powder inhaled through the nose.

while the house was burning and was then found more than a mile away. Another zemi called Epileguarita, made of wood with four feet, often fled from the place where he was worshiped to the woods, and with adoring supplications, they brought him back to the small temple they had built for him. After the Christian Spaniards arrived, that zemi fled and was never found again; this was a harbinger of the loss of their country, as the elders interpreted it. Another marble zemi that those people worshiped was female, and two male ministers had care of her. One of them had the duty of praying to her and to the other zemis, who assist the reigning female, to raise winds, clouds and rains. Another zemi, they say, at the command of the female, would cause the waters to descend from the high mountains and to gather in the valley like rivers, and to run across the fields and ruin everything, if the people did not reform and worship in the proper manner. We relate another great thing worthy of record which those islanders said, that is, that there had been two kings, one of whom, named Guarionex, was already mentioned. For five days in a row he did not eat or drink, and this was in order to obtain grace from the zemis in order to learn things about the future. As a result of his fasting, the following grace was granted to him by his zemi: he said to the king that not many years would pass before a people wearing clothes would come to the island and would destroy their faith, customs, and ceremonies, all of which would completely pass away, and they would be made servants and deprived of all of their property. The young people thought this referred to the actions of the Cannibals, so that when they heard that the Cannibals had arrived at their shores, everyone fled fearing that that event might be taking place; for this reason they feared facing the Cannibals in battle. But when they saw the Spaniards arrive at their island, they all gathered together and concluded that this was the people whom the zemis had prophesied; and the zemis truly did not speak in vain, because since the Christians arrived, all have been converted to Christianity, and those who resisted have been killed, and there is no more mention of zemis since they were all taken to Spain so that their demons and their falsehood be made known. One could say many other things about them, but this is enough for now.

32

PETER MARTYR OF ANGHIERA

On Tainos, Caribs, the Flora and Fauna of the Indies, and the Golden Age of Life According to Nature

1511

Peter Martyr of Anghiera (ca. 1457–1526), an Italian humanist, served as chaplain at the Spanish court. Although he never set foot in the New World, Martyr was well positioned to observe the events following Columbus's return from his first voyage; in addition he claimed to be a friend of Columbus and at one point claimed to be using Columbus's personal writings. He recorded his observations and theories in letters to friends and patrons and in the eight decades or sections of his work De Orbe Novo, *compiled between 1493 and 1525. In these selections from the first decade, published in 1511, Martyr sets out what he has heard about the peaceful Tainos and the ferocious Caribs; he refers to the latter as Cannibals and praises the former with a reference to the theme of a golden age of life according to nature.*

They learned by hearsay that not far from those islands [Hispaniola] are the islands of wild men who feed on human flesh [see Figure 7]. They mentioned afterwards that this was the reason that they had fled in such panic at our arrival; they thought we were Cannibals. This, or Caribs, is the name they give to those savages. They had left the islands of these repulsive creatures behind them to the south, more or less halfway on their journey to these islands. The gentle natives complained that the Cannibals caused constant distress to their islands with their frequent raids for plunder, like hunters attacking and ambushing game as they pursue it through the woods. They castrate the boys they catch, in the way we do roosters or pigs, if we want to rear them to be fatter and more tender for the table; when as a consequence the boys have become large and fat, they eat them. When fully mature men come into their hands, they kill them and divide them into portions; they make a feast of their guts and their extremities

---

Geoffrey Eatough, ed. and trans., *Selections from Peter Martyr,* Repertorium Columbianum 5 (Turnhout, Belgium: Brepols, 1998), 46–47, 67–69.

Figure 7.   *Cannibals of the West Indies.*
This very early representation of cannibalism in the Indies depicts a tranquil group of Caribs feasting inside an open-sided hut; human remains hang from the rafters to cure. The Caribs are portrayed in native dress, but with European physical characteristics. (German woodcut, ca. 1505)

while they are fresh; they pickle their limbs in salt, as we do hams, and preserve them for later occasions. Eating women is for them a sin and disgusting; if they do acquire any young women they tend them and confine them, just as we do hens, ewes, heifers and other animals, to breed from them. They keep the old ones as slaves to be at their service. In these islands, which we can now call ours, when they have forewarning that the Cannibals are approaching, the only safety for men as well as for women lies in flight. Although they use reed arrows sharpened to a point, they have discovered they are of little use in repressing the violence and fury of the Cannibals. For all the natives confess that ten Cannibals would easily overcome a hundred of the others if it came to a battle. They have not fully explored what these two peoples worship apart from the sky and its shining bodies. As for the remaining customs of the islanders the shortness of time and lack of interpreters did not allow them to learn more.

The gentle ones use root crops for food similar in size and shape to our turnips, but the sweetness of their taste is like delicate chestnuts. They call these *ajes* [sweet potatoes]. There is also another kind of root which they call yuca [cassava, manioc]: from this they make a bread. They use the *ajes* roasted or boiled, rather than as a staple for making bread. The yuca however they first cut and squeeze (for it is juicy) then they pound and cook it into cakes. But this is what is amazing: they say the juice of yuca is more deadly than hemlock; if drunk, it kills on the spot.[1] However the bread from the pulp, as everyone has experienced, is tasty and good for you. They also make a bread from some cereal not very different from the millet which is very abundant among the people of Lombardy and the Spaniards in Granada. The ear of this is longer than a span, ending in a point, almost as thick as the top of one's arm; the grain seeds are ranged by nature in a marvelous order, they are like peas in shape and substance: white in their immature state, when they have ripened, they become very black, yet on being split are whiter than snow; they call this kind of cereal maize.

Gold has some value with them, for they wear it, separated into extremely fine leaf, inserted in the lobes of their ears and in their nose, which they pierce. When however our men had learned that merchants did not come to trade with them, and that they are unfamiliar with any shores save their own, they began to ask them by signs where they obtained this gold for themselves. As far as they could gather, using signs, this had been collected with no great toil from the river sand which rolls down in rivers from high mountains: they separated it into little balls, before drawing it into strips, but not in the part of the island controlled by this king, which later experience made clear. For after they had left there, they stumbled by chance upon a river; they leapt ashore to take on water and to fish, and came to the conclusion that there was lots of gold mixed in with the river's sand.

· · ·

While the admiral [Columbus] was listening to divine service on the shore, they noticed one of their chief men; he was an octogenarian and an important man, but, for all that, naked, with many in attendance on him. He stood by in wonder, his eyes and face intent, while the service was being carried out; then he presented the admiral with the gift of a basket, which he was carrying in his hand, full of his

---

[1]The tubers of the yuca plant contain prussic acid.

country's fruits, and sitting in the admiral's presence, with the interpreter Diego Colón,[2] who understood their language since they were near to his home, the man made the following speech: "News has been brought us that trusting in your powerful hand you have voyaged to these lands until now unknown to you, and have brought no ordinary fear to the people living there. I warn you then to be aware that souls have two paths when they leap forth from the body: one gloomy and hideous, prepared for those who cause trouble and are the enemies of the human race; the other delightful and pleasant, appointed for those who in their lives have loved peace and quiet among nations. If therefore you remember you are mortal and that rewards will be duly assigned to each in accordance with his present actions, you will attack no one."

These and several other remarks were translated by the interpreter from the islands for the commander, who was amazed at a judgment like that coming from a naked man. He replied that he was thoroughly informed on all the things he had said about the different journeys and rewards of souls on leaving the body—indeed he had even thought up to this point that they were unknown to the old man and the other inhabitants of these parts, living as they did content with nature. But as for the rest he replied that he had been sent by the king and queen of the Spains to pacify all those shores of the world which had been unknown to this moment, that is, to make war on the Cannibals and any other natives who were wicked men, subdue them and apply the punishments they deserved, but to protect and honor the guiltless because of their virtues; therefore neither he nor anyone else who was not disposed to do harm should fear him. Far from it; they should disclose any injustice which might have been visited on them, or on other good men, by their neighbors.

The commander's words pleased the old man so much that he declared he would very gladly go with the commander, though he was now growing weary with age, and this would have been done, if his wife and sons had not prevented him. Yet he was utterly amazed that the admiral was subject to another man's command, but when he heard an account, through the interpreter, of the magnificence and size of their majesties' ceremonies, their power, their adornments, and

---

[2]Diego Colón was an Indian whom Columbus brought back from the first voyage. He was baptized with his fellow Indians in Barcelona, and given a name that shows his close relationship to Columbus. He is to be distinguished from Diego Colón, Columbus's brother, and Diego Colón, Columbus's son.

their equipment for war, the size of their cities and the splendor of their towns, he was even more dumbstruck. Rather sadly then, his wife and son prostrate before his feet with tears in their eyes, this distinguished old man remained fast, asking again and again whether the sky was the land which produced great men of this character.

It has been discovered that with them the earth, like the sun and water, is common, nor do "mine and yours," the seeds of all evils, fall among them. For they are content with so little that in that vast earth there is an excess of land to farm rather than a lack of anything. Theirs is a golden age: they do not hedge their estates with ditches, walls or hedges; they live with open gardens; without laws, without books, without judges, of their own nature, they cultivate what is right. They judge he is evil and wicked who takes pleasure in inflicting injury on anyone.

33

ALESSANDRO GERALDINI

On Caribs and Tainos

March 29, 1522

In 1488 Alessandro Geraldini (1455–1525) was appointed by Pope Innocent VIII as legate to the Spanish court. He argued in support of Columbus's projected voyage in 1492 and in 1519 was appointed bishop of Santo Domingo, Hispaniola, where he died six years later. Geraldini describes a voyage that begins along the coast of northwest Africa and continues on to the West Indies and Hispaniola.

Finally, on the thirty-seventh day after we had left the Rivus river [in West Africa], with a favorable wind we reached the hateful islands of the Anthropophagi. These people are named Caribs, or "strong men," in their own language; the islands are inhabited by a countless multi-

Geoffrey Symcox and Luciano Formisano, eds., Theodore J. Cachey Jr. and John C. McLucas, trans., *Italian Reports on America 1493–1522: Accounts by Contemporary Observers,* Repertorium Columbianum 12 (Turnhout, Belgium: Brepols, 2002), 116–31.

tude of these most savage people. They emigrated from the island which, as Plato relates in the *Critias,* is larger than Europe and Asia[1] and located 800 miles from the city of Santo Domingo. They ate human flesh, and claimed the mountainous places as their own, where they brought their booty of human captives, and constantly waged war with strong men who abstained from such food, and lived reverently and kindly according to the true law of nature. When they saw that the neighboring islands were unwarlike, they began to cross over to them in many boats, and captured one after another in war, and having taken the males for their unspeakable banquets, they reached the point where they had occupied more than a hundred of the islands of those people, who lived righteously and honorably with a marvelous fairness to all, and eaten all the males on them in their dreadful gluttony. They believe that there are no gods; they are enemies of nature; they are tall and go naked, with very large limbs and altogether savage faces. They use poisoned arrows, the tips of which are made of fish bone, harder than any iron, and so that their long, black hair does not hinder their aim by swinging around their shoulders, they tie it in a knot on top of their heads. Carrying many arrows in their left hands, and constantly rising high with leaps from side to side to avoid being killed by our men's artillery and arrows, they go into battle with their bodies naked and painted with various colors; once they have shot their arrows, they run with incredible speed to nearby woods, of which there is a great abundance on all sides, and when least expected, they return to attack their enemies with incredible force with new arrows and poison. All the neighboring islands were in immeasurable fear and incredible turbulence of mind about their manner of life, and far-off peoples kept look-outs on the highest points of their countries, or on the promontories which project furthest out to sea, who immediately announced their arrival to the neighboring peoples. The Caribs eventually took the bodies of those they had captured in war and, if they were plump, they roasted them hanging from large trees on poles, or boiled them in large pots made of clay, first cutting off their heads and discarding them; if they were too thin, they stuffed them with various rich foods, as we do with fowls which we are saving for a feast-day. Something must be said about the captive children: the pitiless men make them all eunuchs immediately, and after they have fattened them up, they gather them on a holiday of their country and make them sit in the middle of their circle, the poor crowd of children, the wretched

[1] A reference to the lost continent of Atlantis.

troop of humans fattened for food. Then one of the Caribs (for "carib" is a noble name among them: it means, as I said before, "man strong in war") walks around the pitiful flock of children with many gesticulations of his arms, with many contortions of his pitiless face and many body-movements and an altogether fierce expression, twisting his body around them with a cruel look, and then, with a single slash of his wooden sword, which is as sharp as if it were made of hard steel, he cuts off the heads of this one or that, as many as he pleases or has been decided on by the whole group. Then, as a great cheer from the abominable men follows, they celebrate a feast-day, a day filled with pleasure, on the flesh of children fattened beyond what is human. They spare the female captives, and keep them as maids for their wives and servants for their children. They often invoke demons but do not address prayers to them or to any other god; they enjoy thievery and constant war with their enemies, and they consider anyone who does not eat human flesh their enemy. However, they live in admirable peace among themselves: they elect magistrates who quickly remove all conflict from within the whole nation. When they are captured, they always render very faithful service; but I pray all pious mortals and implore the whole race of humane humanity to refuse their service entirely, to avoid the service of men swollen with the flesh of other humans: for since even all of the wild monsters of the world spare their own kind, what good can there be in this kind of human, which does not spare its own? . . .

I have collected so many and such great things, most holy Father, to tell you about the land of this country, that if I had wanted to write everything with proper judgment, I would have needed an immense volume; for it is such a matter that no single human life could be long enough for the task, and no one would believe it unless he saw it in person. Now I must go on to describe the inhabitants of the country. Most blessed Father, the people who lived near the island of Hispaniola were very gentle, and lived by the law of nature, they inflicted no violence on anyone, and they respected the institution of marriage; the highest law of justice and goodness was fixed in their innocent minds, not because of any compulsion, but simply by the goodness of their characters. Those gentle people had petty chiefs, who went out in public with their faces intentionally broad and plain, just as they came from their mothers' wombs, so as to seem even more admirable to their people, and the people treated them with marvelous respect, and never waged any wars except to protect the king's boundaries; they owned everything in common except their houses and shops; their foods were simple; their drink was water; they made bread from roots, which last a long time once they are sown and provide wholesome food for the whole population, though the liquid pressed from them brings death. They also have some types of reeds, from the joints of which grow branches with white clusters of beans, as large and round as chickpeas, from which they make a hearty bread, nourishing food for strong stomachs: they ate this bread with large crabs and lizards, or with fish caught in the ocean or rivers and ponds, or with tiny rabbits. They had boats, carved out of one piece of wood with sharp stones and excellently crafted but long and too narrow, and for that reason very dangerous, which they used for fishing at sea or on the rivers; however, the people ran no real danger because they were expert swimmers: when they were overturned by the heavy billows of the ocean, they dove with incredible speed and brought the boats back to the surface of the sea. They believed that the soul was immortal, and thus there was no mourning for the dead among them; they received public oracles from their gods, who were very dreadful-looking: their hellish gods in fact demanded to be feared, not loved; their ancestors however acknowledged that there was one beginning, one king of heaven, earth, and sea, as their old kings told me. Shortly before Columbus's arrival, they had begun a war with the Anthropophagi, who, having consumed both the nearby and the distant islands in their unspeakable gluttony, crossed over to prey on my people in various kinds of boats, and my islanders, having assembled a countless multitude of men, ran to meet them with poisoned arrows, slingshots, long pikes, and stakes with their points sharpened by fire; then those of my people who were captured were carried off from their homeland and served up in the cruel banquets of the Caribs, or else were revived and saved for the special festivals of the land; the Anthropophagi who were captured by my islanders, on the other hand, were put to a simple death, and their bodies committed to the earth: so great was the natural, innate mercy of my people! Yet those mild people have been treated with such savagery that some of them, with their wives, children, and whole households, have been forced to move ancient rivers from their beds to extract gold from them, with almost no food except for a few fish, and have died at the task; some were exhausted by the long labor, and for that they were riddled with wounds; pregnant women, to whom some lenience ought certainly to have been shown, were forced to perform much harder tasks than their strength allowed, and died after miscarrying their infants; some of the men were carried off to remote mountain areas, surviving only on crab meat, and dropped dead at their work, either giving up the ghost suddenly because no rest was allowed them, or else quickly succumbing to those who were appointed as overseers for these wretched people and killed them by driving swords into their bellies. Everyone in that amazingly populous region was thrown into panic, and as the people fled into the remotest mountains, the bread made from roots gave out, and the grain which had been brought from Baetica was barely sufficient for the people of Spanish origin, and the whole situation was tragic; even the chieftains and the men of the highest nobility were stripped of their possessions and breathed their last amid harsh tortures, as they were forced to confess where their gold, which they did not have, was (gold was in fact one of the things owned privately among these people). Thus, to avoid such cruel slavery, countless men put themselves to a violent death, together with their wives, children, and whole households: for those mortals, from the common teaching of their forebears, judged that disgrace was worse than any death, and they thought that death was nothing, since the soul does not die. I might add that many of our Spaniards slaughtered the unarmed forms of those innocent men on the slightest pretext; nor is this surprising: many men journeyed to that part of the world at the time when those lands were discovered who were already notorious to all humanity for their crimes of theft, murder, embezzlement, larceny, or sacrilege, or those who did not dare go out in public in their homelands because of their mutilated ears[2] or other members, or who could not stay at home because of their well-known crimes against people. These things and many others were committed in such a way, that a million people were killed. And now, most holy Father, those unspeakable mortals, who were so savage to naked, unarmed men who lived by nature's laws, flee for sanctuary to Christian churches; and since all merciful, holy, fair-minded men of the whole church are appalled that these atrocities were committed against the human race, against a race of men whom the name of Christ had never reached but who were innocent of all crime except that one, which was atoned for in a way that disgraces the human race, they are afraid to absolve those men, and the people are in great affliction on account of this, and therefore, it would be an excellent work for you, vicar of the eternal God, shepherd of the Christian people, you who preside over our treasured faith, to order, in consideration of the kinds of troubles and the hardships of these poor people, and the immense quantity of gold

---

[2] A Spanish punishment for thieves and other criminals.

which the Spaniards have extracted from the individual sufferings of these much-afflicted men, that they give me a certain amount to build a cathedral, and establish a major shrine of holy Mary in the city of Santo Domingo, to help spread the name of Christ in this part of the world, where it has never been known before; I will place the church under the direction of men whose religion, integrity, piety, and God-fearing way of life are well respected by the people. I will see to it, with that zeal which becomes a church's governor, and using all the care which is fitting for a Christian officer, that the church becomes extremely famous, and people will flock to admire it from the whole equatorial region, and mortals from the whole land of the Antipodes, who have never seen a Christian church at any time or heard of Christ God in any age (and yet are not far from here), and may they be brought by love to our faith; and all the nations of Europe, Asia, and Africa will cross the sea to this region to see the church;[3] and when they see your holiness's name carved in the walls, and the insignia of the Roman See preserved there, they will praise your holiness fervently, because you will have accomplished such a noble work in a region far distant from the whole upper world. . . . Therefore, most blessed Father, sponsor this church, which will be visited by the whole world and which will be built in your holiness's name: in it will be seen the supreme ornament of your great pontificate, the ultimate monument to your family, and the glorious name of your homeland, so that God the best and greatest may protect your holiness upon the pinnacle of the Christian people for a very long time to come. . . . 29 March 1522.

[3]Geraldini believed that the West Indies were close to East Asia.

A Christopher Columbus Chronology
(1451–1506)

1451   Christopher Columbus is born in Genoa, Italy.

1469   Fernando of Aragón and Isabel of Castile marry.

1474   The crowns of Aragón and Castile are united.

1476   Columbus arrives in Portugal for the first time.

1477   Columbus moves to Lisbon, Portugal.

1479(?)   Columbus marries Felipa Moniz Perestrelo.

September 4, 1479: Treaty of Alcáçovas between Portugal and Spain is signed.

1483–
1485   Columbus tries and fails to receive the support of King João II of Portugal for a voyage of discovery.

1485   Columbus moves to Spain with his son Diego, born ca. 1480; his wife Felipa had died by that time.

1486–
1487   A commission convened by Fernando and Isabel examines Columbus's plans.

January 1486: Columbus is received by Fernando and Isabel at Alcalá de Henares and presents his plans for a voyage of discovery.

August 1487: Fernando and Isabel tell Columbus that the commission has not approved his plans.

1487–
1488   The Portuguese navigator Bartolomeu Dias sails around the Cape of Good Hope, reaching the Indian Ocean.

1488   *August:* Birth of Fernando Colón, the natural son of Columbus and Beatriz Enríquez de Arana.

1492   *January 2:* The reconquest of the Iberian Peninsula ends with the occupation of Granada by Fernando and Isabel.

March 31: Fernando and Isabel sign a decree ordering the Jews of Spain either to be baptized or to leave the country by July 31.

April 17: Fernando and Isabel grant to Columbus the Capitulations of Santa Fe.

August 3: Columbus sets sail, with three ships, from Palos, Spain, on his first voyage.

October 12: Columbus lands on the island of Guanahaní, in the Bahamas, and names it San Salvador.

December 24–25: Santa María is shipwrecked.

1493 *January 16:* Columbus sets sail on his return voyage, leaving thirty-nine Spaniards at the newly established settlement, La Navidad.

March 15: Columbus reaches Palos, Spain.

September 25: Columbus sets sail, with seventeen ships, from Cádiz, Spain, on his second voyage.

November 3: Columbus reaches Dominica.

November 27–28: Columbus reaches Navidad, on Hispaniola, and finds that it has been razed and the men killed.

December: On Hispaniola Columbus chooses the site for the settlement of Isabela.

1494 The French invasion of Italy leads to Spanish intervention and war.

April 24–September 29: Columbus explores the south coast of Cuba and Jamaica.

June 7: The Treaty of Tordesillas between Portugal and Spain is signed.

1496 Bartolomé Colón founds the city of Santo Domingo on Hispaniola, the oldest continuous European settlement in the Americas.

March 10: Columbus sails back to Spain with two ships.

June 11: Columbus arrives in Cádiz, Spain.

1497 *May 20–August 6:* John Cabot sails roundtrip from Bristol, England, to the northern peninsula of Newfoundland.

1498 *May 20:* Vasco da Gama reaches the southwest coast of India, after sailing south and east around the Cape of Good Hope.

May 30: Columbus leaves from Sanlúcar de Barrameda, with six ships, on his third voyage.

August 1: The Spaniards land on Trinidad.

August 5: Columbus sends two boats to land on the South American mainland.

1499 *May 18:* Amerigo Vespucci embarks on the first exploration after Columbus's of the coast of South America.

1499–
1500 *November–September:* Vicente Yáñez Pinzón sails from Palos to Brazil, explores the Amazon, and returns to Palos.

1500 *April 22:* Pedro Álvares Cabral lands on the coast of Brazil.

August 23: Francisco de Bobadilla, appointed by Fernando and Isabel, arrives in Santo Domingo and seizes Columbus's private quarters and possessions.

October: Columbus and his brothers are sent home to Spain in chains.

December: Fernando and Isabel release Columbus.

1501 *September 3:* Queen Isabel appoints Nicolás de Ovando royal governor of the Indies, in succession to Columbus.

1502 *April 15:* Ovando arrives in the Indies to serve as governor until 1509.

May 9: Columbus sets sail, with four ships, from Cádiz, Spain, on his fourth voyage.

1503 *June 25:* Columbus is marooned on Jamaica.

1504 *June 29:* Columbus and the other survivors leave Jamaica and return to Hispaniola.

September 12: Columbus sets sail for Spain.

November 7: Columbus arrives at Sanlúcar de Barrameda, Spain.

November 26: Queen Isabel dies.

1506 *May 20:* Columbus dies in Valladolid, Spain.

Glossary

adelantado   Governor of a province

agnus dei   A small religious medal stamped with the figure of a lamb, honoring Jesus, "the lamb of God"

aje   A sweet potato

almadía   A wooden canoe

arroba   A unit of weight equal to 11.5 kilograms

astrolabe   A compact instrument used to observe the celestial bodies for timetelling, navigation, and astrological purposes

Ave Maria   A prayer in honor of the Virgin Mary

axi   Capsicum; red or chili pepper

blanca   A small copper coin

bohío   A word meaning "house," used by the Tainos to indicate the island on which they lived

bohuti   A seer or prophet; also a type of medical practitioner

cacique   A Taino chieftain

cahiz   A grain measure equivalent to 4.78 metric tons

castellano   A gold coin worth 490 *maravedís,* or 1.31 Venetian ducats; the Venetian ducat weighed 3.5 grams, so the *castellano* weighed approximately 4.6 grams.

Cathay   An old name for China, especially northern China

Cipangu   The Chinese name for Japan

ceuti   A Portuguese coin; 3 *ceutis* equaled 1 *blanca*

cohoba   A hallucinogenic powder inhaled through the nose

corregidor   The royal magistrate or governor of a city in Spain or in the Spanish colonies

cross-staff   An angle-measuring instrument consisting of a rod or staff and a sliding cross-bar, used at sea to determine the angle of celestial bodies *cruzado*   A Portuguese gold coin of approximately the same weight (3.5 grams) and fineness as the Venetian gold ducat, which was the international standard

encomienda   A grant entitling a Spanish colonist to the labor of a group of Indians, supposedly in return for instructing them in the Christian faith

excelente   A gold coin worth two *castellanos,* or 2.62 Venetian ducats, at the time of Fernando and Isabel

fanega   A unit of volume varying between 225 and 555 liters

Guards   The stars Beta and Gamma of Ursa Minor, farthest from the North Star

hidalgo   A member of the lower nobility of Spain

Indies   The West Indies, the islands enclosing the Caribbean Sea between southeastern North America and northern South America

maravedí   A unit of accounting in Christian Spain; 375 *maravedís* had the value of a Venetian gold ducat

marco (mark)   A weight approximately equal to 230 grams

real   A Portuguese silver coin of about the same weight (3.5 grams) as the Venetian gold ducat

reboans   A wooden drum

rubbio   A unit of dry measure (about 194.4 liters) used to weigh sugar at Madeira

Salve Regina   A hymn in honor of the Virgin Mary

zemi   An idol; a Taino spirit or supernatural being

Questions for Consideration

1. The term *globalization* describes the increasing interdependence of the world's diverse regions and their economies. What part did Columbus's voyages play in this process?

2. Why did the Portuguese crown reject Columbus's proposal for a westward voyage to Asia? Why did the Spanish crown accept it?

3. To what extent were Columbus's voyages and the Spanish colonization in the Americas that resulted from them the continuation of medieval commercial and colonizing practices in the Mediterranean and Iberia?

4. To what extent were Columbus's voyages motivated by his Christian faith, and to what extent did religious factors determine the Spanish crown's support for them? What other motives—commerce, rivalry with other European powers—were involved? In what ways were the motives connected?

5. Why did Columbus's voyages lead to permanent European settlement in the Americas, whereas the tenth-century Viking voyages did not?

6. What does Columbus's Log tell us about his first impression of the peoples he encountered and of their reactions to him?

7. Why did relations between the Spanish colonists and the indigenous peoples of the Indies deteriorate so rapidly? What were the consequences for both the indigenous peoples and the colonists?

8. How did Columbus's relationship to the Spanish crown change over time, and why?

9. Is it possible to arrive at a balanced understanding of Columbus's voyages using the European sources we possess, in the absence of documentation from the Tainos or Caribs?

10. Assess the significance of European maritime technology and superior weaponry in making the Enterprise of the Indies possible.

11. Analyze the consequences of the exchange of food plants, animals, and diseases among Eurasia, Africa, and the Americas after 1492.

12. How was Columbus's achievement judged by his contemporaries? How has the assessment of the man and his voyages changed over time, and why?

13. Some historians argue that we should no longer use the term *discovery* to describe Columbus's 1492 voyage or the term *Indians* to describe the people he encountered. Why are these long-accepted terms now being criticized? Is this criticism valid?

14. Why was Christopher Columbus adopted as a national hero in the United States, and what role has he played in the formation of the nation's identity?

Selected Bibliography

PRIMARY SOURCES

Carrillo, Jesús, ed., and Diane Avalle-Arce, trans., preface by Anthony Pagden. *Oviedo on Columbus*. Repertorium Columbianum 9. Turnhout, Belgium: Brepols, 2000.

Cummins, John. *The Voyage of Christopher Columbus: Columbus's Own Journal of Discovery, Newly Restored and Translated*. New York: St. Martin's Press, 1992.

Davenport, Frances Gardiner, ed. *European Treaties Bearing on the History of the United States and Its Dependencies*. 4 vols. Washington DC: Carnegie Institution of Washington, 1917–1939.

Dotson, John, ed. and trans., and Aldo Agosto, ed. *Christopher Columbus and His Family: The Genoese and Ligurian Documents*. Repertorium Columbianum 4. Turnhout, Belgium: Brepols, 1998.

Dunn, Oliver, and James E. Kelley Jr., eds. and trans. *The Diario of Christopher Columbus's First Voyage to America, 1492–1493*. Norman, OK: University of Oklahoma Press, 1989.

Eatough, Geoffrey, ed. and trans. *Selections from Peter Martyr*. Repertorium Columbianum 5. Turnhout, Belgium: Brepols, 1998.

Gallinari, Luciano, ed. *Diego Alvarez Chanca, Medico di Cristoforo Colombo*. Cagliari, Italy: Istituto sui Rapporti Italo-Iberici, 1992.

Griffin, Nigel, ed. and trans., intro. Anthony Pagden. *Las Casas on Columbus: Background and the Second and Fourth Voyages*. Repertorium Columbianum 7. Turnhout, Belgium: Brepols, 1999.

Lardicci, Francesca, ed., Cynthia L. Chamberlin and Blair Sullivan, trans. *A Synoptic Edition of the Log of Columbus's First Voyage*. Repertorium Columbianum 6. Turnhout, Belgium: Brepols, 1999.

Nader, Helen, ed. and trans., and Luciano Formisano, ed. *The Book of Privileges Issued to Christopher Columbus by King Fernando and Queen Isabel 1492–1502*. Repertorium Columbianum 2. Berkeley: University of California Press, 1996.

Phillips, William D. Jr., ed., Mark D. Johnston, philologist, and Anne Marie Wolf, trans. *Testimonies from the Columbian Lawsuits.* Repertorium Columbianum 8. Turnhout, Belgium: Brepols, 2000.

Rusconi, Roberto, ed., and Blair Sullivan, trans. *The 'Book of Prophecies' Edited by Christopher Columbus.* Repertorium Columbianum 3. Berkeley: University of California Press, 1997.

Symcox, Geoffrey, and Giovanna Rabitti, ed., Peter D. Diehl, trans. *Italian Reports on America 1493–1522: Letters, Dispatches, and Papal Bulls.* Repertorium Columbianum 10. Turnhout, Belgium: Brepols, 2001.

Symcox, Geoffrey, and Jesús Carrillo, eds., Michael Hammer and Blair Sullivan, trans. *Las Casas on Columbus: The Third Voyage.* Repertorium Columbianum 11. Turnhout, Belgium: Brepols, 2001.

Symcox, Geoffrey, and Luciano Formisano, eds., Theodore J. Cachey Jr. and John C. McLucas, trans. *Italian Reports on America 1493–1522: Accounts by Contemporary Observers.* Repertorium Columbianum 12. Turnhout, Belgium: Brepols, 2002.

SECONDARY SOURCES

Bedini, Silvio A., ed. *The Christopher Columbus Encyclopedia.* 2 vols. New York: Simon and Schuster, 1992.

Chiappelli, Fredi, ed., and Michael J. B. Allen and Robert L. Benson, co-eds. *First Images of America: The Impact of the New World on the Old.* Berkeley: University of California Press, 1976.

Crosby, Alfred W. *The Columbian Exchange: Biological and Cultural Consequences of 1492.* Westport, CT: Greenwood, 1973.

Davidson, Miles H. *Columbus Then and Now: A Life Reexamined.* Norman, OK: University of Oklahoma Press, 1997.

Fernández-Armesto, Felipe. *Columbus.* New York: Oxford University Press, 1991.

Flint, Valerie I. J. *The Imaginative Landscape of Christopher Columbus.* Princeton: Princeton University Press, 1992.

Granzotto, Gianni. *Christopher Columbus.* Stephen Sartarelli, trans. Garden City, NY: Doubleday, 1985.

Greenblatt, Stephen. *Marvelous Possessions: The Wonder of the New World.* New York: The Clarendon Press, 1991.

Henige, David P. *In Search of Columbus: The Sources for the First Voyage.* Tucson: University of Arizona Press, 1991.

Irving, Washington. *The Life and Voyages of Christopher Columbus.* 1828. John Harmon McElroy, ed. Boston: Twayne Publishers, 1981.

Morison, Samuel E. *Admiral of the Ocean Sea: A Life of Christopher Columbus.* 1942. Reprint, New York: Time Inc., 1962.

Morison, Samuel E. *Christopher Columbus, Mariner.* 1955. Reprint, New York: New American Library, 1983.

Nebenzahl, Kenneth. *Atlas of Columbus and the Great Discoveries.* Chicago: Rand McNally, 1990.

Pagden, Anthony. *The Fall of Natural Man: The American Indian and the Origins of Comparative Ethnology.* Cambridge, UK: Cambridge University Press, 1986.

Parry, John Horace. *The Age of Reconnaissance.* 1963. Berkeley: University of California Press, 1981.

Phillips, William D., Jr., and Carla Rahn Phillips. *The Worlds of Christopher Columbus.* Cambridge, UK: Cambridge University Press, 1992.

Sale, Kirkpatrick. *The Conquest of Paradise. Christopher Columbus and the Columbian Legacy.* New York: Penguin Books, 1991.

Taviani, Paolo E. *Christopher Columbus: The Grand Design.* London: Orbis, 1985.

Viola, Herman J., and Carolyn Margolis, eds. *Seeds of Change: A Quincentennial Commemoration.* Washington, DC: Smithsonian Institution Press, 1991.

Watts, Pauline Moffat. "Prophecy and Discovery: On the Spiritual Origins of Christopher Columbus's 'Enterprise of the Indies.'" *American Historical Review,* 99, no. 1 (February 1985): 73–102.

Wilford, John Noble. *The Mysterious History of Columbus: An Exploration of the Man, the Myth, and the Legacy.* New York: Knopf, 1991.

Zamora, Margarita. *Reading Columbus.* Berkeley: University of California Press, 1993.

Index